Jehangir H Kothari

Impressions of a First Tour Round the World, in 1883 and 1884

Embracing travels in Europe, the United States of America, Canada, Japan, China,

the Straits settlements, and the northern portions of India

Jehangir H Kothari

Impressions of a First Tour Round the World, in 1883 and 1884
Embracing travels in Europe, the United States of America, Canada, Japan, China, the Straits settlements, and the northern portions of India

ISBN/EAN: 9783337172145

Printed in Europe, USA, Canada, Australia, Japan

Cover: Foto ©Andreas Hilbeck / pixelio.de

More available books at **www.hansebooks.com**

IMPRESSIONS

OF

A FIRST TOUR

ROUND THE WORLD

IN 1883 AND 1884.

EMBRACING TRAVELS

IN

EUROPE, THE UNITED STATES OF AMERICA, CANADA, JAPAN,
CHINA, THE STRAITS SETTLEMENTS, AND THE
NORTHERN PORTIONS OF INDIA.

BY

JEHANGIR H. KOTHARI.

[FOR PRIVATE CIRCULATION.]

LONDON:
1889.

PREFACE.

At the earnest solicitations of many valued friends, both in England and in India, who have expressed an interest in my FIRST TOUR ROUND THE WORLD during the years 1883 and 1884, I make my first adventure in authorship. I have complied, not without some misgivings, knowing my inability to completely realize all that may be expected of me.

I have embraced in the present diary my travels through Europe, the United States of America, Canada, Japan, China, the Straits Settlements, and parts of Northern India, and in giving my views and impressions fully and unreservedly of the various places which I have visited, and of the characteristics, manners, and customs of the different peoples I have seen, I crave the indulgence of the reader for any errors of judgment I may have committed. I am now on my Second Tour Round the World, and should this account of my First Tour be sufficiently appreciated, I may be induced to publish the results of that Tour also, which will include Australasia, and various other interesting parts of the globe.

I am not without some hope that my desire to interest the reader may be in a measure realized by my first effort.

JEHANGIR H. KOTHARI.

LONDON,
   June, 1889.

CONTENTS.

	PAGE
EUROPE	1
SCOTCH TOUR	155
BRITISH TOUR	174
IRISH TOUR	211
UNITED STATES OF AMERICA	226
CANADA	244
JAPAN	263
CHINA	275
STRAITS SETTLEMENT	282
PORTIONS OF NORTHERN INDIA	284

IMPRESSIONS OF A FIRST TOUR ROUND THE WORLD,

IN 1883 AND 1884.

1883, *May* 1. It was on a fine May evening that I started, at 5 p.m., per the British India Steam Navigation steam ship "Oriental," Captain Lewins, on my travels to the New World. The weather we experienced on the first night was not encouraging, as the sea was very rough; indeed, so much so, that even "old sailors" amongst my fellow-passengers found themselves compelled, with pale faces, to enter their cabins, and get through the night the best way they could. The next morning we had a better sea, and all of us were on deck, happy and bright as possible. One of our passengers was the Nawab of Lucknow, who was returning with his brother, wives, and household, from Mecca. We reached Bombay harbour on the night of the 3rd, at 10 p.m. We were agreeably surprised on our arrival to find that a friend of ours was awaiting us in a boat alongside the steamer at such an hour of the night; he prevailed upon us to go with him to the city. Our fellow passenger, Dr. Archer, was with us at the time, and he being unwell, we took him to "Watson's Hotel." After that, we made for the "Waverley," where a treat of champagne was awaiting us, kindly provided by our friend. We then drove round Bombay and saw the sights worth seeing. At night the view of Bombay harbour and the town from Malabar Hill is very fine. We returned to the steamer at 3 a.m. In the course of the day we bade good-bye to our relatives and friends, and went on board the fine Peninsular and Oriental steamer "Malwa," Captain Loggin, for Suez.

May 4. Fairly off! Good-bye India for a short time. The weather through the trip was favourable and most enjoyable. The Captain was one of the most sociable and agreeable men I ever met. He did all he could to make our passage as lively and happy as possible; in fact, he did not leave a stone unturned —or, I should say, a rope untwisted—to add to our amusement in the way of private theatricals, nigger minstrels, sports, concerts, etc.

I must mention one or two of the amusements we had. Mr. Beadon, of the Bengal Civil Service, was the prime mover among the passengers. Mr. Ashwood and his companions (of Dave Carson's

Company) were hunted up among the second-class passengers, and added any amount of fun to the theatricals by their Christy Minstrel songs and jokes. The engineers and stewards of the vessel also assisted in this entertainment. I must not forget to mention the Red Sea sports, got up by Mr. Beadon, General Edwards, Justice Kemball, and others. The most interesting of these sports—which, by the bye, lasted three days—was an animal race; dog, sheep, monkey, cock, hen, pig, etc., were all duly entered and handicapped. The race was eventually won, after roars of laughter, by a sheep. Ladies also joined our sports; we had a button-hole, skipping, and threading the needle race.

May 10. We sighted Aden at about mid-day, and went on shore at 2 p.m. No sooner had our steamer entered the harbour than hundreds of Somali boys, in their little boats, crowded round the vessel and offered to dive after a two-anna piece. It is quite extraordinary to watch these divers; no sooner had we thrown the coin into the water, than the youngster, say of ten years of age, plunges down and brings the coin out with him, usually in his mouth. The first impression I had of Aden was very good. The crescent-like shape of the harbour, seen more distinctly by rows of houses and shops built upon it, is very beautiful; but, like most oriental towns, the charm ceases as soon as you enter the place. The streets are miserable, the houses poor and badly built. After having taken a drive about, we went on a small hill called the "Steamer Point," where the Peninsular and Oriental Company have their buildings, etc. We dined here with Mr. Mermanjee, who was very courteous and kind during our short stay. We left Aden harbour at 9 p.m. We were most fortunate in our passage through the Red Sea. Up to this date we were told on all sides what terribly hot weather we should have through this sea—most likely also rough weather; but I am glad to say they were all false prophets. The weather was beautifully mild, the sea quite calm, and the passage, therefore, quite delightful. We came across two wrecks, and passed them very closely, and discerned the names. They were both steamers, "The Gulf of Finnland" and a West Indian trader. We passed Shadwen Island May 14. 7 p.m.

May 16. *Suez.*—Arrived 10 a.m. Consternation came on every one when informed that we could not land, but that the Egyptian Government had ordered quarantine to be made for three days. The Captain did all he could to get us off, produced a clean bill of health; but it was of no use. The mail bags were fumigated and taken ashore, and we were ordered off to Moses' Well, about five miles off Suez, and to anchor there. The passengers consulted with the Captain, and it was finally arranged to request Mr. Roberts, Agent of the Peninsular and Oriental Company, who was alongside the vessel, to telegraph to Alexandria that there was no cholera in India, and that, furthermore, there was not one case of even ordinary sickness on board. This was done, and the following day we had a telegram from head-quarters at Alexandria, ordering the Egyptian authorities to give us free pratique. As soon as we got this notice we left for the Docks, and landed. We then found ourselves astride the famous Suez donkeys, and made our way through the town. The streets are narrow, and the buildings in French style. Any number of cafés, concert rooms, etc., are to be seen here. We visited the English and Egyptian telegraph offices, and, lastly, the fresh-water canal and the Victoria Hospital, the nicest spot in Suez. This hospital is built on piles, and has all around a very fine garden; in fact, it is a very beautiful spot. We returned to the steamer for dinner, and then made for the station, *en route* by rail for Alexandria.

Left Suez at 10 p.m. by the Egyptian sleeping-car. We had supper at Zagazig. Saw Kasassin, Tel-el-Kebir, Tanta, Kafir-Daur, and finally arrived at Alexandria at 11 a.m. on the 18th. I was sorry I could not see the ruins of Alexandria; but, unfortunately, as we were delayed a day in consequence of the quarantine business at Suez, no time was allowed us. We arrived alongside the Peninsular and Oriental steamer "Mongolia" in the train, and had to go on board at once. In fact, we had only been on board about fifteen minutes when orders were given for us to start. The passengers that had arrived by other routes on their way home were also delayed a day, and had to wait for us.

May 18. Off Alexandria. Here we had pointed out to us the various forts held by Arabi's troops during the bombardment of Alexandria, amongst them the famous Fort Marabout, where Captain Beresford distinguished himself so much in the "Condor." We were really then steaming through the same waters in which the terrible English fleet lay, and in about nine hours demolished these strong forts. We also saw, on quitting Alexandria harbour, the "Inflexible," the "Falcon," and the Turkish ironclads. It was the Khedive's feast day, and all the ships in dock were decked out in bunting.

The "Mongolia" is one of the best ships on this line, and we got comfortable berths on deck, although they were aft. The weather we had was, on the whole, good, but not as calm a sea as we had in the Red Sea. I don't think I shall have much to say about the three days between Alexandria and Brindisi. The passengers were very dull and quiet, about one hundred and twenty in number, so the time lay somewhat heavily on our hands. It was only on the last evening that a small attempt was made at a concert. The Captain called up the engineers and stokers, who were all Italians, to sing a few songs, which they did very well indeed, and certainly proved to us the talent of their nation, for, after all, they were only men of the common order.

The following morning,

May 20, arrived at Brindisi, after having gone through a heavy fog at sea all the morning. Brindisi is a small place, and not very busy. I think that if it were not for the connection of steamers with the railway as the nearest way to England, it would be of little significance. We took our tickets to London, and drove in a cab, drawn by two smart ponies, to the station, where after a little waiting and a little pulling about, which seems customary in Italy, we got into the Pullman car for Bologna. The contrast between our Indian cars and that of the Pullman is so great, that, on entering it, I must say I was very much struck with its magnificence and comfort, and made up my mind to describe it as fully as I can. The name is after its inventor and maker, an American, who holds a patent for it. The car itself is about as long as three of our ordinary Indian cars. It is divided into three compartments. These three are placed in the body of the car, and allow a margin all round the whole of the car, which is called the verandah, and is used as a smoking compartment. The first division is, during the day time, a very fine saloon, with splendid velvet cushion seats all around, to seat sixteen passengers. The panel decorations, lamps, brackets, etc., are perfect; in fact, when seated in this compartment, I could imagine myself in a first-class drawing-room. During the night the scene in our saloon changes completely. The conductor, who has a special small room at the end of the car, comes in and starts unfolding our seats. The back of the seat flaps downwards, the side is thrown over, the under part of the seat draws out. He covers the mattress over, gives us a good pillow, sheets, and blanket; and here is our seat transformed into a first-rate bed. And when he has done all the beds, you look around, and can imagine yourself on board ship, in an enormous cabin holding thirty-two beds. There is an arrangement to draw silk curtains right round each bed, so that you have, so to say, a small room to yourself. There is a special compartment for ladies in the same style. Nothing in this wonderful car has been forgotten which might add comfort to the passengers; lavatories, elaborately arranged, are found at the back of the car, on either side, for ladies and gentlemen respectively.

Sunday morning, we are in the train, ready to start for London without break of journey, and have one thousand seven hundred and fifty miles before us. The great question to those passengers who have not booked by the mail train, which can only accommodate a few passengers, is, "Will we be in time for the Derby?" One of these unfortunates, a planter, was so excited about getting home in time for the race, that he was running about the Brindisi Station, offering ten guineas for an exchange of ticket of the sleeping-car train for that of the express ; he did not find a seller. It is just as well he did not, for we learnt eventually that he had backed the wrong horse.

We rattled away at a very good speed through Ancona, Bologna, Turin, Mâcon, Dijon, to Paris, stopping only a few minutes at the divers stations. There is nothing to describe except the beautiful country we passed through, especially between Turin and Modane, the French frontier. Close to the latter place we pass the beautiful Italian mountains, the height being covered with snow, and in the valley the waters rushing down as the hot sun is gradually melting the snow. We have passed through the Mont Cenis Tunnel, a grand piece of workmanship and engineering. It is only on looking back towards the huge mountain behind us, that we can realize the greatness of the work.

At Turin we had to quit the mail train, as we had not reserved sleeping-car tickets, and wait for the next express to Paris. Here we had lunch, a good wash, which was a great treat, as the Italian roads are so dusty. An hour later we were on our road to Paris for Calais.

We arrived in Paris at 9 a.m., had another wash

(another great treat), and a good breakfast, and started from Paris at 10.30. We crossed the Channel on board the "Invicta," the best steamer on this line, and built with all the improvements of the day. She is rather a small steamer, paddle; but the size of her engines are enormous, and she runs, on the average, sixteen knots. She is fitted with electric light, and a very fine saloon, which can accommodate about two hundred passengers.

We arrived, after a run of seventy minutes, at the Admiralty Pier at Dover, and were at six o'clock in "Old England." We took the South Eastern express train to London, and arrived at Charing Cross at 8 p.m.,

May 22. Went into the hotel which is in the station, and considered one of the best hotels. I adopted the suggestion of my friends to lunch and dine at various hotels and restaurants during my stay, so that I might visit and see as much as possible. We therefore dined this evening at the Grand Hotel. This hotel is a new one; it was built in 1878, at a cost of two hundred thousand pounds. The ironwork used in this building cost twenty thousand pounds. The saloon is a very grand one, and the electric light shows the saloon to great advantage. Dinner and attendance good.

May 23. We got up early, and started off at eight o'clock from Charing Cross Hotel to Regent Street, by cab. It would be very hard for me to explain what impression the first sight of London streets, and life, and traffic made upon me. All seemed to me so large, and the speed with which we went through the streets did not give me much opportunity of realizing all I was seeing and passing.

We first entered a shop, and "rigged" ourselves with veils, sticks, gloves, etc., for the Derby. In Regent Street we found our carriage and pair waiting, and, together with Mr. Jobbling, we drove to his house, and from there, after his family had joined us, we were off for the Derby. The drive to Epsom is sixteen miles. We could have gone by train; but in order to see the scenery, and the well-known Epsom road on Derby Day, we chose a drive,

The road is one of those sights I will never forget. From the costermonger's donkey-cart to the nobleman's drag (four-in-hand), and from the nigger minstrel to the prima donna at Her Majesty's Theatre, all were making headway towards the scene of the great event.

On arriving at the course, the scene is almost indescribable. The thousands of people, nay, tens of thousands, of all classes crowded round so small a space is certainly a wonderful sight. We took up an excellent position on "The Slope," where we commanded a view of the whole course. The well-known fun that I have read about, the tricksters, betting-men,

I here saw in reality. All kinds of strolling minstrels, all kinds of games, such as one may see at a fair, were going on here.

During the small races which preceded the Derby, we had lunch. Mr. Jobbling had prepared a very first-rate lunch, which was contained in no less than eight hampers. I must not forget that I was fortunate enough to make the acquaintance of Sir John Bennett, Major Furnival, and Mr. Barrington, of theatrical fame, who joined us at lunch.

We got up a sweep, and I drew St. Blaize. The jockeys of the great race are now on the course, the place is in great bustle; all are shifting to the best positions they can secure. "Here they are! see them! They are off! there they go! St. Blaize!" is the cry. The race is over. The excitement during the race itself is immense; in fact, terrible.

We returned the same way, after having our photos taken by a strolling artist on the course. We dined at a restaurant called the "Criterion," the property of the well-known Spiers and Pond. This restaurant is most perfect in its arrangements : on the lower floor you can be served by American barmen with American drinks, or by English girls with English drinks, or by French waiters with Paris coffee, etc. ; on the same floor there are also elaborate luncheon rooms. We dined in the saloon, which is very grand indeed. The dinner was good.

May 24. Went to the Grand Lodge of England, visited Colonel Shadwell Clark, the Grand Secretary, and was introduced to Mr. Maudslay; went to our Bankers, and in the evening dined at the Holborn Restaurant in what is called the Venetian saloon, which is decorated in very grand style, lit up by electric light, and in which a band plays during dinner hours. After dinner we went to the Gaiety Theatre to see "Blue Beard"; it was very amusing.

May 25. We breakfasted at a very good restaurant, St. James's, and then went on to the Royal Academy, Piccadilly. The building of this Academy is very grand indeed; it is in the shape of a horseshoe, and from what I understood, is used for exhibiting the pictures of painters and the work of other artists executed during the year. No old pictures and work are exhibited here. I was very much interested, and was sorry that I could not devote more than five hours to it. The pictures were beautiful. I saw paintings by Millais, Frith, and many other eminent artists. It was rather unfortunate that the place was very crowded, and I could not get a view of everything that I should have liked to see. Many pictures and statues that I saw were most exquisite, and the busts and portraits comprised all the eminent men of the day.

Went to the City, and on my way inspected Trafalgar Square. This covers a very large space, and is, I think, the largest open space in London. It is, so to say, dedicated to Lord Nelson, for in the centre there arises an enormous granite column about one hundred and fifty feet high, which is crowned by a statue of the great hero. Four colossal bronze statues of lions, modelled by Landseer, form the pedestal to this monument, which run out from it in the shape of a cross. There are also two small fountains on either side of this square, and at the extreme ends two statues, one of Sir H. Havelock, and the other of Sir Charles Napier.

I now come to the City—the great City of London. Well may they call it great and busy. The continual and most extraordinary bustle and traffic is quite sufficient to bewilder the ordinary stranger; on the footwalks the business people seem to rush along as if for a race; carts, drags, omnibuses, and crowds of other vehicles, completely fill the streets. It is here that you can see that time is money. Returned to hotel.

May 26. Called upon Messrs. Thomas Cook and Son. Mr. Cook himself was away in America; was introduced to his manager, Mr. Cates; spoke to him about a trip on the Continent. We had lunch at Crosby Hall, in the heart of the City. This restaurant was at one time the palace of King Richard III., and is mentioned in Shakspere. We had lunch in the throne room. The old style of building is still to be seen, as the place has only been renovated and decorated. Went back to the West-end, had tea at the Café Royale, and dined later on at the St. James's Hall. This is a very fine dining saloon; there is a band in attendance during dinner hours. The dinner was good, but not as good as at most of the other places I went to. After dinner we went to the Adelphi Theatre and saw Charles Warner in the tragic play "Storm-Beaten." I thought this play was nice, indeed, and affecting.

May 27. Went to Brighton, and after having taken lunch at the Grand Hotel, we went to the promenade on the pier, which was crowded with people, and presented a scene of a most lively and active description. This pier is one thousand one hundred and fifty feet long, and at the end of it, although it was Sunday, a band was performing; I enjoyed this very much. We went on to the Aquarium, with which I was delighted. There are here forty large tanks, which hold great numbers of fish, etc., of the most curious and interesting description. I also saw seal, sea lions, alligators, etc. From here we returned to the hotel for dinner, and then went on to the town, where we took a carriage for a drive round. Returned to station and took the midnight train for London.

May 28. Visited the extensive premises of Messrs. Manger and Son, Musical Box and Watch Manufacturers. Lunched at the Greek restaurant, where we had an oriental dinner, and were served altogether in the Greek fashion. Drove to the Empire Club, where I was proposed as member by the secretary, Mr. Fagg, and seconded by Viscount Bury. Here we had dinner, and then went on to the Savoy Theatre, where we saw the well-known performance of " Rip Van Winkle."

May 29. Called upon Messrs. Ross and Matthews, the tramway contractors. Visited the nursery gardens at Cremorne, which is a huge plot of land covered with nurseries and hot-houses. Lunch at Gatti's, near hotel. We then went to see the performance which is got up for the yearly benefit of the Benevolent Society; this performance is always gone through by the greatest actors of England. We saw here, in "Shylock," Henry Irving and Miss Terry. "The Rivals," Farren and Henry Neville. "Money," Hare, Miss Ada Cavendish, Mr. and Mrs. Kendall; also the great Toole, who amused us immensely—in fact, all actors were of the best. This was a morning performance; it began at 1 p.m. and was over at 6. Dined again at the Holborn, and went on to the London Aquarium. This is not as good as that in Brighton, but we had, besides the tanks of fish, etc., other performances and shows. A waxwork exhibition was one that struck me most: on entering I saw a female figure balancing a ball on a stick, which was on her forehead; the movement of the body (the work of the wax) was in all so splendid that it looked exactly like life. This building cost two hundred thousand pounds, and is six hundred feet long; it includes salt and fresh water tanks, a summer and winter garden, theatre, concert room, picture gallery, and restaurant.

May 30. Went to Hyde Park, and for the first time, I here saw the Prince of Wales, at the meet of the four-in-hand club inside the park. The turnout of this club is to me beyond description. What beautiful horses; how everything is looking bright and happy; what good driving. This sight was, in reality, superb. It is needless to say that the park was swarming with people, for it is here that the nobility once a year show off their horses together. We visited the Fisheries Exhibition at the Horticultural Gardens, Kensington. This being an international exhibition, we saw here, from almost all nations in the world, some kind of representative. We saw of the divers nations their different methods of catching fish: Dutch, Danish, German, French, and even Japanese. Huge fish caught at the English fisheries were exhibited, and sold to the public at very low rates. The fish I saw was very fine indeed, enormous salmon glittering like silver. We walked then into the gardens, which were beautifully laid out, and also to the building containing the tropical plants. In here it is like what one would imagine fairyland to be. Palms of all kinds and sizes, bananas, cactus in every shape and form, and all other foreign trees and plants are to be found here. The band of the Life Guards was performing here. After lunch we went to the concert at the Albert Hall; this was in aid of distressed soldiers and seamen, and was patronized by the Queen and the Duke of Cambridge. This hall is oval in form, and is, I think, one of the largest in the world, as it can accommodate eight thousand persons easily; it is two hundred and seventy feet long, and two hundred and forty feet across, and cost two hundred thousand pounds. The place is lit up by no less than seven thousand gas jets, and the organ, which stands at the end of the hall, is the largest in the world. It has eight thousand pipes, and its bellows are worked by two steam engines. The concert was delightful; we heard the greatest singers of the day, foremost being the wonderful Adelina Patti. We visited Prince Albert's Memorial in Kensington Gardens, which is facing the Albert Hall. This magnificent monument to the late Prince Consort was erected at a cost of one hundred and twenty thousand pounds. Mounting a lot of granite steps, we come to a large square block of marble, adorned with the figures of the great artists of every period on all its sides. At the angles of this square are four very large statues, representing Agriculture, Manufacture, Commerce, and Engineering. In the centre of this block sits the colossal gilt figure of the Prince Consort. This monument is gorgeously embellished with bronzing, marble statues, mosaics, etc. At the corners of the steps below, leading to the monument itself, are four pedestals bearing very large figures, representing Europe, Asia, Africa, and America. Leaving the monument, I drove to the City and entered the new Law Courts. This is an immense building, which has lately been opened to the public, and is not quite complete yet. It cost over a million pounds to build. I went into the Court, and the various judges I saw were the Lord Chief Justice of England, Justices Manisty, Lopes, Matthews, Chitty, Denman, and Brett. I also heard a little of the "Belt" libel case. I then went to the great printers, Cassell, Petter, and Galpin. I inspected the whole process of lithographing, engraving, stereotyping, and printing. The place is quite enormous, and the courtesy I received at their hands in showing to me and explaining all that was to be seen and learnt was very great. Their large printing room is a grand sight, there were over forty large printing machines in full action, besides a quantity of smaller ones: over the whole of their building they employ about eleven hundred hands. The quick way in which the girls were folding the enormous sheets printed, amused us very much.

June 1. Visited the extensive premises of the Masonic and Jewel Manufacturer, G. Henning, and had conversation about Colonel Shadwell Clark's

Lodge. Dined at the Criterion, and visited the Trocadero Palace Theatre.

June 2. Not well.

June 3. Went to Lee, Kent; drove round beautiful country, and dined with Mr. Warwick; returned to London at 4. Called on Mr. Boyce and family at Hammersmith, and spent the evening with them. Returned per railway to London.

June 4. Called on Mr. Wortley and Bankers. Dined at Holborn, and went to Drury Lane and saw the play, " Youth."

June 5. I am now packing my trunk to be off for a Continental tour, and start from Charing Cross Station, *viâ* Dover and Calais, for Paris, by the 10 a.m. train. The ride to Dover is a very beautiful one, as the line passes through the finest English country. After a run of about two hours, we arrived at Dover. The train stops alongside the pier, and hence we embarked on the " Invicta " again for Calais. It was fortunate that we caught the boat, for, as I said before, she is the fastest on the line. The sea was not calm, and the ship rolled a good deal, in consequence, as the sailors affirmed, that the tide was with us, and the wind against the ship. All around were pale faces, which gradually grew paler and paler until most of the deck passengers found their way below. We kept, however, very fair time, and were off again from Calais, after having taken some soup, for Paris, where we arrived, *via* Boulogne and Amiens, at 8 p.m. Here we drove to the Grand Hotel, had a good wash, and went down to dinner, or, I should say, supper, for it was past nine o'clock. After dinner, we walked out on the boulevard for half an hour, and went to bed, being rather tired.

June 6. Paris being the largest town in Europe that I have visited, with the exception of London, it is natural that I should, in trying to describe it, make my comparisons with London. As we go through the streets and watch all around us, we find the ways, customs, and manners of the people, and the general aspect of everything, so vastly different to anything English, that, considering the short distance separating these two countries, it is quite astounding. The streets here are not as we have been in the habit of seeing them in London, narrow and smoky. They are beautifully wide, with grand-looking mansions built on either side of the road, four and five, some six and seven stories high. They look bright and clean, and are built in bold and very artistic style. Most of the streets, called boulevards, are lined with trees, and this gives the place in general a very fine aspect. I do not think that in my travels I shall come across so fine a town or city as Paris. The municipality here do not seem to wish to spare any trouble or money in making everything look as grand as possible. It is true that the French nation has always been used to most lavish expenditure under the Kings and Emperors reigns, which, no doubt, has spoilt them. The Grand Hotel is situated on the Boulevard des Capucines, which is considered, together with that of the Boulevard des Italiens, the finest street in Paris. It is a most enormous block of building, belonging to a French banking company, and is furnished and decorated in the most elaborate style. The French are fond of external decoration, such as gilding and bronzing, etc., and in going through the rooms and apartments of this hotel, the traveller is much struck with the richness of all around him. The room I occupied was a very large one, overlooking the grand opera house; its furniture was very handsome, rich carpet, grand chandeliers, any amount of pier and looking glasses, sideboards, flower stands, etc.; but here we see the Frenchman. All he cares for is outward show, he does not study comfort. A towel horse is considered in England an indispensable piece of furniture in a bed-room, but with the Frenchman this is too ugly-looking an article. The washing stand is small and pretty, but comfort requires a large one, and a big basin instead of a pretty little decorated arrangement. A toilet table is also not supplied here. In the house itself the bath-rooms are not as the English would have them, close to the bed-room. It is true that when you get there, after, say, ten minutes' journey round a lot of passages and up and down staircases, that the bathroom is very fine and elaborate ; but still, this is not comfort. The reading rooms, drawing-room, billiard, smoking, and other rooms are here worth visiting as really grand sights, each one being furnished and decorated in different style, and all with such exquisite taste that is peculiar to the French nation. We now went for a drive through the grand boulevards of the town, and had to keep admiring the beauty of all around. About five minutes' drive brings us to the Place de la Concorde. This place is, undoubtedly, the grandest place or open square I shall ever see.

This square, which covers an enormous space, has in the centre a large obelisk, of the same shape as, but somewhat smaller than, Cleopatra's Needle. It was brought to France by Louis XV., and its erection, etc., cost over eighty thousand pounds. On either side of this obelisk, at a distance of about eighty yards each way, are two beautiful fountains. They consist of a circular stone basin, fifty feet in diameter, surmounted by two smaller basins. Six enormous figures are seated around it, with their feet on the prows of vessels, and from the centre of the basin six huge dolphins are spouting out water. The top basins are overflowing into the lower one from water spouted from the very top of the fountain. The square is enclosed with balustrades, which are broken at various intervals by huge figures representing the eight provincial towns of France, viz., Lille, Bordeaux, Nantes,

Rouen, Marseilles, Lyons, Brest, and Strasburg. This latter town having been annexed by Germany, the female figure representing this town has been decorated by the public, not with flags, as the others, but with wreaths of everlasting flowers and black ribbons. It is on this spot that on the marriage of Louis XVI., one thousand two hundred persons lost their lives in a panic that had arisen in consequence of a fire that had broken out close by; and also on this spot this poor King lost his head under the guillotine. It is on this spot that the monstrous plots of the Commune were arranged, and through whom thousands of people lost their lives.

From here we drive up the Champs Elysées, the grand and fashionable drive of Paris, which is planted with beautiful trees on either side, and on the spaces beyond the trees gardens are laid out in good style. Visited the Panorama in the Champs Elysées. This represents the defence of Paris on the last line of fortifications during the Franco-German War. It is a painting erected in circular shape, and arranged in such a way that the figures, buildings, and forts look exactly as if you were on the spot. The picture gives one a good idea of the horrors of war. The dead men being carried away, the wounded attended to, and the others firing and protecting their forts are most remarkably natural.

We returned to the Champs Elysées and entered

the Galérie des Beaux Arts. This was part of the building erected for the Great Paris Exhibition, and since then bought by the Government and used as an academy of fine arts. The exhibition going on was that of the yearly work of the French artists, something similar to the Academy in London, and is called the "Salon." The paintings, on the whole, were very good indeed; but in comparing this with the London Academy, I think I liked the latter best. The peculiar tastes of the Frenchman here show themselves—he is fond of choosing horrible subjects, executions, murders, all kinds of assassination and bloodshed, and then, again, nude pictures are his delight. Also, all the horrible men in France—such as Marat, Danton, Robespierre—are to be found here in numbers, either as portraits or busts. Still, taking it on the whole, the exhibition is a splendid one.

We returned to the hotel for dinner. The dining saloon at the Grand is grand. The place will hold over eight hundred seats comfortably; the decoration, service, electric light, and music which is in attendance, adds immensely to the beauty and luxury of the saloon. This must be one of the finest public saloons in the world, if not the finest. The dinner was very good. There were over two hundred at dinner.

We now went off to the Hippodrome. This building is very plainly built of iron girders, with a large glass sliding roof, which in good weather is rolled aside, and the public is under open air. The hall is of very large dimensions, and is the largest circus in the world. It is lit up by the electric light, and the performance consisted of flat, chariot, and Olympian races, as well as the usual acrobatic and circus performances. I was very much pleased with the entertainment.

I omitted to mention that at the end of the Champs Elysées I inspected the famous Arc de Triomphe, which was planned for erection by Napoleon I., and was erected in honour of the "Grande Armee." It was commenced in 1806, and, after being stopped for some time, was finally completed in 1836. This proud monument consists of an arch ninety feet high and forty-five wide, over which rises a bold square structure, making the total height one hundred and fifty-two feet.

The whole of this colossal arch is covered with inscriptions of the names of the victorious French generals and the different battles they fought. Four groups of statues adorn the sides of this arch, the most important representing Victory crowning Napoleon ; Fame surmounts the whole statue, and History records his deeds. At his feet are the names of the vanquished towns ; and the whole of this work was done by the greatest masters of the day, and cost over four hundred thousand pounds.

June 7. Inspected Colonne de Vendôme. This

monument was erected by Napoleon I. after his war with Germany. It is a column one hundred and thirty-five feet high and twelve feet diameter, and is covered with bronze work weighing one hundred and fifty tons, and cast from the guns captured from the enemy. The statue of Napoleon is on the top of this column. It was pulled down by the Communists in 1871, and was re-erected after the Republic was declared.

We drove on to Notre Dame. This Cathedral is a very grand building, the entrance presenting a great quantity of sculpture, which consists of two very large porches. The buildings around the Cathedral are too close to get a proper view of it. The interior struck me very much. The enormously high roof is very finely built and beautifully decorated. There are two very large windows, built of stone and arranged with coloured glass, which are very fine indeed. We entered the treasury of this Cathedral, where we saw the gold service used at the coronation of Napoleon I., the cup out of which Marie Antoinette drank before she was beheaded, and several other gold and silver services of enormous value; also the robes of the Archbishops, which are embroidered in gold and adorned with precious stones; most gifts of the Kings and Emperors of France to the church.

We crossed the square, and went to visit the "Morgue." This is a place in which the bodies of unknown persons who have met with death are deposited for three days. They are laid on inclined slabs of marble, open to the inspection of the public. Their clothes are hung up near them, an additional means of recognition. The bodies are separated from the public by glass screens. I saw five bodies—two men and three women. A large quantity of photos of unknown bodies are hung up in the place.

Saw the Statue of Joan of Arc, and the Garden of the Tuileries, which is a very fine park ; also the ruins of the Tuileries, which was barbarously burnt down by the Commune in 1871.

Dined at Hotel Continental, which hotel, again, is one of those elaborate places that Paris alone can produce. The dinner was excellent, and the service seemed better than that of the Grand ; so that I made up my mind to leave the latter, and take up my stay here, which I did the same evening. We then went to a concert on the Champs Elysées, called the Ambassadeurs. There is no charge made for admittance ; but you are supposed to drink something, and the price charged for same is such as will fully counterbalance the free pass. We heard comic songs in French and English, saw acrobatic performances, etc., which was very good.

June 8. Mail day. Wrote all the morning, and dined at the Maison Dórée, which is well known as one of the old-fashioned Paris restaurants. In the evening, went to the Eden Theatre. This is another specimen of the gorgeous way in which Paris builds its theatres and hotels. The place is built in Alhambra style, and is shaped as an ordinary theatre, with the exception of a very wide promenade on the three sides. The decorations are magnificent, and the arrangements very good. An extravaganza in five acts was represented, and very well mounted, the ballet being very fine. During the *entracte* the public promenade, and a band, consisting of about fifteen girls, conducted by a portly dame, amuse the public during this usually slow gap in other places of amusements. I enjoyed this evening very much indeed.

June 9. Visited the Palais Royal, which at one time was the palace and garden of the Kings of France, but is now converted into an immense arcade and square of shops. We had lunch here, and then went on to the Louvre.

The Louvre is the largest building in Paris, and is the Museum of the Nation. Here we entered, and I was astonished with the magnificence of it. We went from one gallery to another, inspecting pictures, statues, porcelaines, gobelins, bronzes, the Naval Museum, the Egyptian, the Assyrian, and other Museums. From one department to the other, one did not know what to admire most. The treasures here represent millions of pounds, and this Museum is, as one block, the largest in existence. To lay particular stress on any picture or pictures, I cannot; for I saw so many painted by the Old Masters, Titian, Raphael, Michael Angelo, and others, whose single picture is a treasure in itself, and, as regards value, represents a fortune. The departments of the China, particularly that of the Sevrès, were most exquisite; and here, again, in such quantity that one did not know where and what to admire most.

The relics brought over from Egypt and Nineveh are most interesting. An enormous sphinx, of solid granite, must have cost enormous labour and a great deal of outlay to bring over.

We dined at the Hotel des Louvre, another of these grand Parisian hotels. The dinner was very good, and served in the same style as the Grand. The saloon is not so elaborate as that of the Grand; but still it is very fine indeed, and decorated in good taste.

Here we drove to the Theatre Châtelets, where a French drama, "Kleber," was being performed. I did not understand the language; but from what was translated to me, I could follow the play very well, and was much pleased with the acting and the *mise-en-scene*. The play represented the life of the famous General Kleber, who fell in Egypt, and laid the foundation stone to the rise of Napoleon.

June 10. This morning we went to the St. Lazare

Station, *en route* for an excursion to Versailles. The train takes a little over an hour, and passes, in going round the City of Paris, where one can get a good view of the different monuments, through a very picturesque country, studded with beautiful villas belonging to the *grande monde* of Paris. On arrival at Versailles, we went to the Hotel de Reservoirs for luncheon. This place has become famous since the Franco-German War; for in the same saloon in which we had our luncheon, Bismarck, Moltke, and all the grand Generals of the German Army were in the habit of dining; and, finally, at the treaty of Paris, they met here in this very same saloon to make arrangements with the heads of the French Army to put a stop to the horrors of the French Commune.

Hired a cab, and drove out to see Versailles and its glories. This town has always been the great favourite of the later Kings and Emperors of France, and it was only in the last few years of the reign of Napoleon III. that Versailles lost some of its royal patronage. The avenues of Versailles, as we must call them, show still the traces of ancient grandeur; although they are still very handsome, they present a neglected aspect. They are lined with magnificent trees, trimmed to a square shape. As we turn one of the corners, the coachman points out to us the house in which Ferdinand de Lesseps was born. A humble-looking building; over the doorway a tablet is placed, saying he was born in this house, with the date, etc.

We now pass a long and beautiful alley of trees, and reach the Palaces of the Trianon. The first was built by Louis XV. for Madame de Maintenon. The first impression one has of this palace is very poor. It is a one-story building, in horse-shoe shape, and looks as if it had no roof; but it is not until we are fairly inside that our opinion changes as to its merits. We pass from one handsome apartment to another: the Boudoir, the Bedroom, the Grand Bedroom of Louis XIV.; and here we have before us a most elaborate piece of furniture, the real bed in which Louis died. The bed is very fine indeed; but the fact that he died in this bed did not make any great impression. The spot facing this bed, and near the window, is the place where Louis XV. breathed his last, seated in his chair.

We now go down again and enter the exhibition of Carriages. These are all the State Carriages of the Kings and Emperors. They seem everyone to wish to excel the other in grandeur. One would imagine that the most magnificent one built for Louis XIV. would have been good enough to satisfy the desire of the most lavish of monarchs. Not a bit of it. He himself was not pleased with the first one, and had a second one made, which cost the State no less than twenty thousand pounds. Napoleon I., however, not satisfied with this, thought he might add to the magnificence of the latter; he built one that cost double that money. It is made of bronze, in the old-fashioned C spring style, and is very heavily gilt. It is adorned with flowers and small figures in the most elaborate style, from designs by the best masters of the time. A number of other carriages is also here, the one of most interest being that which served to conduct the unfortunate Louis XVI. and poor Marie Antoinette to the Cathedral on the occasion of their marriage. Poor Louis! it was a different vehicle which conducted him to his rest. There are also a number of sledges here, all belonging to the crowned heads of France.

We go next to the Grand Trianon. This is also a palace, built in exactly the same style as the other, and which is, in most cases, similar to the last palace. The apartments of Marie Antoinette are very interesting: here we are in the boudoir of this unfortunate woman, with all the furniture in it which she used at the time; here is her dressing-room, the very bed she slept in, her bedroom, and the sofas and chairs of her small reception room, all in keeping with the modest demands of this unhappy woman.

We now pass through a suite of chambers of the King: the library, dressing-room, drawing-room, and bedroom, of Louis XVI. These were only the apartments used by Royalty for a very short time during the year, and were not their actual palaces, but, so to say, their country residence.

We now return to the town to see the real palace. This is called Le Palais de Versailles, and in order to form an idea of the size of the place before entering, it has on its front and sides three hundred and seventy five windows, and cost forty million francs to build. The old entrances are now done away with, as it seems they would not be suitable for allowing the public in and out. We find on the first floor the State apartments of Louis Philippe (afterwards Louis XIV.), then Louis XVI., and the Napoleons. We first come to the billiard rooms, the table used by Royalty; these are not as good as those to be found now in the small cafés of Paris, with the exception of the wood carving of the legs and sides of the table. The decorations of the ceilings are, one and all, through the whole of this palace, of the most elaborate style possible, and in each case the subjects shown are in keeping with the purpose for which the room or saloon was intended.

From the billiard room we come to the divers reception rooms, the gentlemen's rooms, the ladies' rooms, the concert saloons, and finally we reach the dancing saloon. I can quite understand where the money went to when I am standing here. This saloon has over thirty windows in it, and is the largest room I have ever seen—two hundred and forty feet long. The walls are decorated in relief in the same elaborate style we are getting so used to see here. The ceilings in themselves are, every corner of them, works of art.

The flooring, which is of wood, is something magnificent—in fact, this saloon is perfectly dazzling in its grandeur. We also see, further on, the reception rooms and ante-chambers, and then, going on to the next wing, the private apartments of the Queen. The grand saloon faces the Park of Versailles, and in the centre saloon there is a large balcony, on which Marie Antoinette stood when she was imploring the infuriated mob for mercy. As we go through the private apartments here we are told that Marie Antoinette, when she saw that all her begging was in vain, ran and shut herself up in her rooms. Here we stand now in those very apartments. They are very small, and with low ceilings, and very poorly furnished compared with the grandeur of those of the King. Her little boudoir, her library and small chapel, and, lastly, her little bedroom.

In passing through these apartments a pang must strike the heart of every visitor when he thinks over the history of this ill-fated Queen, and more especially of the last and troublesome moments she must have spent here. They show us the secret way through which she made her escape, and the spot on which the brave Swiss men were murdered who were protecting her, and who gave away their lives in order to give her a minute's more time to escape. What a humiliation it must be to every Frenchman going through this part of the palace to think over the history of the barbarous Revolution. I felt quite angry with the guide who showed us round, and it made me all the more so as he repeated his tale off by heart without the slightest feeling. Of course, we don't expect him to cry ten times a day over this sad tale, but there are many ways of telling it.

We are glad to get out of these sad reflections into the open air, and find ourselves in the most magnificent park and gardens imaginable. This, indeed, is one of the glories of France. The whole of this lovely park and gardens surround the palace, and in coming out of the main entrance, down a grand staircase, the view is delightful, for we look down upon one mass of green lawn in the centre, forming a very broad alley, and called the *tapis vert*, lined with elaborate statuary, and marble vases in profusion. On either side of the *tapis vert* we have a beautiful park, tastefully arranged with grottos, Swiss cottages here and there, fountains, etc. At other parts the wood is left wild and forms a fine contrast to the gardens surrounding it. All through this vast space we are continually coming upon fountains of all descriptions. The largest of these fountains is that of the Basins de Neptune, formed of five large groups, the centre one representing Neptune and Amphitrite seated in an immense shell surrounded by nymphs and sea monsters. In the centre of the basin is a spout, which forces up the water to a height of one hundred and forty feet, with a volume of about five thousand gallons per minute. This is all I shall say of the park and palace, for to describe it all hundreds of pages would not suffice to do it justice.

To imagine what Louis XIV. did to beautify this place—letting alone the other monarchs after him—it is almost enough to say that he spent fifty millions of pounds over it. The whole of the surrounding country, to an extent of about sixty miles in circumference, was purchased, hills were levelled or created, valleys filled up or excavated, water was brought from a great distance to perfect the landscape. This is what impoverished the country, for the expense of keeping up such a Court can be readily imagined, and this was certainly the cause of the First Revolution, under which poor Louis XVI. and his family had to suffer, instead of that monster Louis XIV.

From the palace grounds we visited the Senate, which, however, under the present Republic, has been transferred to Paris, and is only used now for the election of a new President. It is a large, simple hall, with numbered seats all round. Gambetta's seat, No. 76, was pointed out to us.

All seems deserted here; the town itself, which numbered over one hundred thousand, only holds now scarcely thirty thousand inhabitants.

We are off again to Paris, and have supper at the Continental.

June 11. We start to-day, *viâ* Dijon and Mâçon, for Geneva.

June 12. We stay here at the Hotel Metropole, a first-class hotel. Geneva is beautifully situated at the extremity of the lake, and has about fifty thousand inhabitants.

We went for a drive round the town, and first visited the statue of the Duke of Brunswick, who, by the bye, bequeathed a fortune of about one million sterling to the town. The monument and statue are very elegant and sumptuous, and were built immediately after the Duke's death, in 1873. Visited Rath Museum; very small, but has some fine pictures. We also passed the various places of note, such as the Cathedral, Hotel de Ville, University, Theatre, etc. Visited the Panorama, illustrating the French soldiers in 1870 and 1871 being allowed to enter Swiss territory, after being disarmed by the Swiss soldiers. This panorama is very effective, and illustrated again to us the horrors of war.

June 13 *and* 14. Went for a drive down the beautiful lake; but we could not get a view of the range of mountains before us, as they were covered with clouds. Called upon Mr. Conchon, a manufacturer of musical instruments, who treated us very politely indeed, and showed us all the wonders of his place. There were most elaborate instruments to be seen here of all kinds and descriptions. Purchased some things, and, after having made arrangements for the diligence to take us to Chamounix, we started,

June 15, with a six-horsed vehicle, containing no less than twenty-five passengers, of almost every country, at 8 a.m. The journey was begun with delightful weather, and the road runs along the river Arne, which rushes down the Chamounix valley. After a short drive through the Sardinian frontier, we reached Cluses, a small town well known for the manufacture of Geneva watches. After changing horses and coachman three times, we arrive at Sallanches, a small town; where a halt is made for luncheon (1 p.m.). Here we stay forty minutes, and, after being provided with a very poor meal, change our good horses for a set of very miserable ones, we slowly find our way towards Chamounix. The view all around us becomes more and more interesting; but, unfortunately, the weather having changed, we are trying to look out through the curtains of the diligence, and are stretching our necks right and left to get a glimpse at a waterfall or down the frightful chasms beneath. The other sights above us are hardly visible, in consequence of the weather. Thus, after a hard journey, we arrive at Chamounix, at 6.30 p.m., and take up our quarters at the Hotel d'Angleterre. We are glad to go to bed early, and get up the next morning,

June 16, ready, and with any amount of energy,

to go up part the way to the Monarch of the Mountains—the Mont Blanc.

We ascend through a pine forest the mountain range facing the town of Chamounix. After about an hour's walk, I find it rather toilsome work, and fortunately hit upon a guide and mule on the road, who is ready to take me up to the Hotel at the top of the Mont Auvert. There is a great sameness in this road. It is toilsome, uphill work, rather slippery, in consequence of the rain that fell during the night, and also it is narrow. After travelling a height of six thousand three hundred feet, we reach the top of Mont Auvert.

Here we suddenly see before us—or rather, I should say, beneath us—the so-called Mer de Glace. Is it possible for me to try and describe in vulgar words the mighty and majestic scene before us? I am almost afraid to attempt it.

Here beneath we have a broad stream of ice—or, I should say, a frozen sea—the offspring of the highest Alps, which pours between lofty mountain ridges down into the valley. Looking around us, we see the terrific majestic peaks covered with the glistening snow. One seems to be dreaming. Looking around, the whole view is something grand, beautiful, and terrible. The weather is, unfortunately, bad, and the clouds look more and more threatening every minute. What shall we do? Shall we return the same way? It seems such a pity, once we are here, not to be able to cross the Mer de Glace. We ask our guide, Prosper Payot—who, I may mention, is one of the crack guides here, and who ascended the top of Mont Blanc no less than thirty-three times, and is the only guide who has ever ascended the more dangerous Aiguille de Dru. He says: "It is nothing. Half-an-hour across the Mer de Glace, then an hour's walk to the Chapeau on the other side, and there the mules will meet us." This seemed very tempting; we at last made up our minds to cross, and, having armed ourselves with blankets over our shoulders, which we borrowed from the hotel keeper—I mean the blankets, not the shoulders—we started making our descent. It was so tempting at the start! But by the time I got to the midst of the sea of ice I repented doing so, when I discovered what the nature of it was. One did not only run the risk of slipping and falling, but found himself continually on the brink of ice crevices in an ice-mass of two or three hundred feet deep, over which one must step or almost leap! I was in a state of silent despair at having undertaken such a journey. My guide was very careful with me, but certainly this enterprise was more than I had bargained for, and when, having found ourselves midway on this Mer de Glace, I was asked to notice the splendid walls of ice around and the brightness and width of the frozen sea, I felt more like the man doomed, with the rope round his neck, and desired to view the "fair prospect."

We are over the Mer de Glace, after all! How delighted I was to get again a fair footing on the ground; but again my pleasure was of short duration. We had now to make our way along slate rocks, with slippery grey sand and no path whatever, towards the Chapeau. My guide pointed out the place, after about an hour's walk—or, I should say, climb—and it did not look far away. But nothing in the world is more deceptive than distance is here. On we crawl, till my guide points out that we have reached the Mauvais Pas, which means "bad step." Surely, if all we have gone through has no name, and we are now to have a bad step, what is it going to be?

One walks along a narrow pathway cut in the rock, not an inch too wide for an ordinary sized foot, and beneath us a few hundred feet of slanting rock and the end of the Mer de Glace, called the Glacier des Bois. A moment's dizziness here—a slip, and all would be over! How long this step was! On and on it kept winding round, till at last, after a wearisome and dangerous adventure, I reached the Chapeau, where we found a small hut, and after many a sigh of relief and a good cup of coffee, I mounted the mule, with little strength left to hold on, and descended the latter part of the mountain to the valley. Here a carriage was procured, and after bidding good-bye to Prosper Payot, we drove off to the hotel, which was reached by a flat road along the valley in about twenty minutes. We were very wet, as it had been raining all the while, and I need not say that I was not long taking off my things and finding myself between the blankets. It was now about 6.30 p.m.

June 17. I got up rather late, but refreshed after my previous hard day's work. The weather was very bad to-day, and we did not venture out. This being Sunday, most of the travellers in the hotel being English, went to their church, which is close to the hotel.

June 18. 8 a.m. our carriage and pair is waiting to conduct us to Martigny *via* the Tête Noir. The road being very bad along this pass, the diligence does not run here. We leave the Mer de Glace to our back, and commence ascending the opposite mountains. The weather is fairly good, but the view that we should have of the Mont Blanc range is covered with clouds. Travelling up hill all the way, and after having ascended over three thousand feet, we reach the village of Argentiere. The view here is very fine, especially the glacier of the same name. We now descend somewhat, and the valley contracts, the road running very closely along the edge of the mountain, and the view we have below of a gorgeous wooded ravine, with the stream far below us rushing wildly, is one of the most picturesque scenes I have passed in Switzerland. We ascend again for a time closely to the skirt of the Tête Noir, and pass through a tunnel hewn out of the solid rock which overhangs the valley, and as we pass through this, on our right we have enormous rocks covered with ferns and the top of the mountains one mass of fir trees.

Shortly after passing this short tunnel we halt at the hotel Tête Noir for luncheon, and after two hours' rest continue our journey towards Martigny. The ride is very beautiful, as all the way we are cutting through a pine forest and passing picturesque scenery. We are going up hill all the way until we reach the Col de la Forclaz, where, after having reached a height of about five thousand feet, we begin descending towards the valley. After about half-hour's descent we suddenly have one of the most noble views thrown before us: the whole of the Rhone Valley lies as a map under our feet. The valley is beautiful and green, with a bright sun shining on it, and the river Rhone running in a zigzag the length of it. Immediately below us lies Martigny, and although it seems so near, still it takes us two full hours to reach it. We go to the Hotel de la Poste, a rather dingy-looking house, for dinner, and immediately after it just manage to catch our train for Lausanne, which town we reach at about 11 p.m. Sleep at Hotel Riche Mont, and as there is nothing worthy of note here, we go on to Berne by first train.

June 19. Berne is not so large a town as I expected it to be, and on referring I find it has only a little over forty thousand inhabitants. The city is built on a peninsula formed by the river Aur. We took a drive through the town and first viewed the bridge that is just about being completed across the river. It is very handsome indeed, built of three large iron arches. When all the scaffolding is taken away this structure will compare favourably with any bridge in Europe. The cathedral we visited next. This is a handsome Gothic structure about four hundred years old. The organ is the chief attraction of the cathedral; it is a very famous one, and it was being played upon while we were there; its sounds are very powerful and very mellow. We now went to see the bears' den of Berne, where Bruin is here kept since time immemorial at the expense of the Municipality. It is remarkable how fond they are of their bears; every statue, establishment, or sign, is sure to have a bear upon it in some shape or another. If I lived here I should think that continually seeing nothing but bears all over the town would make it quite unbearable. Only a small drive up the hill, where there is a beautiful garden called the Schamfi, and then off to the station, bidding Berne and its bears good-bye, where we take the train for Lucerne, arriving at 9 p.m. We stay at the Hotel National, a very good and comfortable hotel.

June 20. Morning, write letters, and in the afternoon we take a nice drive round the town, first along the beautiful Schweizerhof quay, with its most handsome mansions and hotels.

We visit now the famous lion of Lucerne, erected, or, properly speaking, executed, in 1821, for this monument is carved out of the solid rock, and represents a dying lion with a broken lance stuck in his body. This is a very simple monument, but its simplicity makes it all the more impressive, for it is placed there in memory of the eight hundred Swiss soldiers and officers who, during the Revolution, defended the Tuileries, and fell in the defence of a foreign monarch. Lucerne must be a delightful place to live in, for its position on the lake is very beautiful, and from the windows of our hotel at night, with a full moon shining on the lake, and on the other side the mountains towering up covered with glistening snow, is a view never to be forgotten.

June 21. We now take the train to Zurich, which we reach at 10 a.m., and from the station at once make for the National Exhibition. We enter a most elaborately decorated portal, in Swiss chalet style, leading to the central department of the manufactures of Switzerland; silks, cloths, cottons, and all kinds of other drapery. A great many of the exhibits are very tastefully arranged, but the close inspection of fashionable dresses and dress material I left to the ladies, who, it is needless to say, were swarming round the cases.

We now pass the musical department—pianos, organs of every size and description. I was very much interested in the piano used by Beethoven. There it stood, a small, simple, unpretending instrument with yellow looking keys, the edges of which were actually quite worn away by the hands of the great master, known to have been so continually upon them.

The next department is musical boxes. Here they were in all shapes and sizes. We use these instruments again and again without hardly ever thinking what an intricate and difficult thing it is to make one.

I was very much surprised and interested in going through the works of Mr. Conchon, at Geneva, where I saw the whole process of their manufacture. The setting in of the small pins in the rollers is a matter requiring the most marvellous accuracy. The roller is first made, then it is taken to be marked ; a man sits here with the music before him, and marks with a fine steel point the different places on the roller where the holes are to be made for the pins. From his hand it passes on to the drilling machine, where the holes are made with the greatest care. Then it passes on to another hand, where the pins are placed in the roller, afterwards passing the delicate inspection made by a woman, who, with the music before her, has to inspect every pin singly, sound it, and hear whether the note is perfect one by one. For every note in the piece a careful examination has to be made of every pin, and if not found quite correct it has to be tapped to its proper position. The patience she must have is undoubtedly great, and can be imagined, when I was told it took her six weeks to adjust one roller for a musical box ordered by the Crown Prince of Prussia.

Here I saw the rough steel and brass, and the uncut logs of wood, which after a short time would represent a handsome musical-box playing away its melodious tunes.

The watch department was also very interesting.

Let us now get back to our National Exhibition, and go through the mechanical department. Here we see all kinds of machinery in motion, chocolate-making, printing, weaving, spinning, and even stockings knitted by machine. This was a most interesting little instrument, worked by a young woman, and by turning a handle she, with the greatest ease and in a very short time, turned out a most beautifully knitted lady's stocking.

We pass a quantity of stalls, containing, mostly, carved wood fancy articles, which the Swiss are so famous for. The pretty costumes the girls wear, who sell at the various stalls, are of the Swiss national costume, and are very becoming.

The natural history department contains, amongst others, a very beautiful collection of stuffed animals and birds of the country. This was a pretty show.

Now we leave the Exhibition for a drive round the beautiful town. I was very much struck with the piles of handsome buildings here, erected, it would seem, regardless of cost. Private houses, looking more like small palaces than anything else, beautiful broad and clean streets, lined with chestnut trees.

The town itself is very well situated on both banks of the small Lake of Zurich, and the hilly and highly cultivated country around helps to add to its beauty. Around us we have to add to this scenery the immense mountains, nine and ten thousand feet high, covered in snow.

After visiting the Munster, the Cathedral, we drive up the hill called the Schauze, where we see the enormous Polytechnic, a rather modern building, and very handsomely and substantially built. From here we command a fine survey of the town, and after this make for the station, where we have a hurried lunch, and just manage to jump into the train for Neuhausen.

We will shortly be over the borders of this beautiful little country. In turning back towards the last few days, one cannot help noticing the contrast between the previous ten days at London and Paris. What a different life here. It is all for the natural wonders that we come here; there, for all the artificial. I only went once to the theatre in Switzerland, and that was at Geneva, where, fortunately, the place was opened for three days only, as Sarah Bernhardt was performing, *en passant*.

She acted that night in the famous play "Fedora." Her acting is, beyond doubt, most excellent; the easy and graceful way she moves about the stage makes her most exquisitely natural. I was so glad I had seen her acting, and I am sure the general opinion is never exaggerated.

We leave Zurich, and go, *viâ* Winterthur and Schaffhausen, to Neuhausen, where, after having a view of the majestic falls of the Rhine, we take the evening train for Strasburg, arriving late at night.

June 22. Hotel de la Maison Rouge. We are now in Germany, which only a few years ago was French. In coming out of the hotel, the shells and cannon-balls that struck the house are pointed out to us; they have been replaced in the wall in the same position that they were supposed to have pierced the walls.

It is very curious to go through a town that has been only recently annexed. The monuments, memorials, and statues are those that belonged to the enemy. Here before us is the statue of Kleber; I now recognize the actor who took his part at the theatre in Paris.

We now take a drive round the fortifications, or, I

should say, part of them; for they are very extensive, and the Germans are still busy strengthening them. Our coachman is a staunch German, and the proud way in which he elaborates every now and then over the victories of his fellow countrymen is quite amusing. "On those hills over there," he says, "our soldiers stood, and it is from there that our artillery did most of their work. Now here you see the gate through which the troops passed when they came in after the capitulation. All these beautiful houses you see here are new; they were all destroyed during the bombardment. You see that quaint-looking old house opposite; that was the only one left standing in the whole of this road, and the shells stuck in its walls are German ones.

"The garrison here consists of about a hundred thousand men now; but of course you know in time of war it would be more than double. The public has not got quite used to being Germans yet, but it will come in time. We are doing a great deal for them. Look how many schools we have built, and presently you shall see the University."

There is no doubt about the truth of this last statement; the Germans seem to be doing their utmost to make the public reconciled to their change. The University is not quite finished yet; but it is the most handsome public building of the kind I have seen. It is enormous in extent, and, when finished, will be found a great boon to the inhabitants. There are a few streets and two large squares that are being made.

We have to go to the Cathedral now. This is a most magnificent structure, and is as yet the finest I have seen. The exterior is built on the most lavish style, every nook and corner carved out in stone, and its high tower, the highest but one in the world, majestically standing erect as if wishing to reach the clouds.

The interior is also most beautiful. The old stained glass windows, in great numbers, are very fine indeed. In one of the wings of the Cathedral stands the famous Strasburg Clock. This is the most marvellous specimen of calculation and intricate work possible. It indicates the day of the week, month, and year; the signs of the zodiac; the moveable feasts; the rising and setting of the sun, the moon, and the different phases of the latter, the eclipses of both; the comets; the movements of all the planets; and has also a church calendar; and the whole of this is indicated by a number of dials, automatically, and set to run for 999 years. The day of the week and the hour of the day are represented by moving figures; twelve o'clock being the most elaborate. The four quarters of the hour are struck by, 1st, the Infant; 2nd, the Lad; 3rd, the Man; and, 4th, the Old Man. These four figures are about twelve or fifteen inches in height, and walk out from the side of the clock towards the bell, which stands on a kind of platform, and, hammer in hand, they strike; they represent the four stages of life : Death then comes walking on the scene and strikes the hour.

After that, on the top of the clock, is a small opening. The figures of the twelve Apostles appear, and pass by a standing figure, representing Christ, who blesses them as they move forward; and when the ninth has passed, on the left-hand side, at the very top of the clock, a large cock flaps his wings and crows three times. The whole of this performance occupies only two and a half minutes.

We now go to lunch at the Hotel, where the General von Bülow, in command of the garrison, was also at the same table, with his staff. He is a fine-looking old man, and, I think, the grandson of General Bülow, of Waterloo.

We start for Heidelberg, which we reach by train in the afternoon, and drive up to the famous Castle. It was such a lovely drive up the beautifully wooded hill. The towers of this castle only now show the ruins of bygone grandeur. Here it was when the " Masters of the country" governed all around them by the sword. The old drawbridges and huge iron gates are still here, but most of the rest of the tower is in ruins. We went down the cellars, and saw the old casks that these revellers used. The largest is forty-one feet high by twenty-eight long, and was actually filled.

We drove round this beautiful city, across a handsome bridge, some distance along the river, and then returned to the station, where, after having dinner, we got into the train for Bingen, arriving there at midnight. Slept at the White House Hotel, and after breakfast went on board the "Humbold,"

June 23, a paddle-steamer, for a trip up the Rhine as far as Cologne.

This was a delightful trip. The scenery around us was all the way of the loveliest. The ruined castles built on the tips of the rocks on the mountains which hang over the river change the scenery to that of the quiet villages below. The Drachenfels is the grandest of these sights on the Rhine; also the Lorelei, a huge black-looking rock overhangs the river and gives a sombre effect to the scenery around.

The boat we were on was very nice and comfortable, and the dinner they gave us was particularly good. We reached Coblentz at about 3 p.m., Bonn at about 4.30 p.m., and finally arrived in Cologne at 6.30 p.m. Stayed at Hotel Disch.

June 24. After breakfast we go to the Cathedral —the famous one which really took about six hundred years to build. It was Sunday morning, and, as there was mass going on, we went in, and were fortunate enough to hear the choir sing. They sang most splendidly. I need scarcely say that is the finest building I have entered.

The Strasburg Cathedral struck me very much, as regards its beauty and grandeur; but this was certainly more than I could ever have thought of. The outside is decorated with carved stone in a very rich manner, and nearly every stone of this colossal mass has been carefully cut and carved. The entrance is covered with little statues intended to represent parts of the Bible, and as we enter it is then I can realize its enormous height. What labour the huge block must have cost, and the expense, have never been ascertained.

We now drive on to the Flora. This is at the extreme end of Cologne, where we enter a very fine garden and an enormous glass building containing all kinds of tropical plants. I then went on to the Zoological Gardens. It was very amusing and interesting to view the excellent collection they have here; the lions, especially, are very good specimens.

We now take the train for Brussels, which is reached the same evening at about four o'clock.

Let me say a few words about Belgium. Taking into consideration the size of this country, that is only about eleven thousand miles area, and its population hardly exceeding that of London, every person will be struck with the great industry of this small country.

The system of railways is known to be the most complete in the world; the out-turn of iron from its hundreds of works is also well known; we can hardly look out of the railway carriage for one moment without passing a factory of some kind. We pass Liege —a perfect forest of chimneys. In fact, as I pass along, it seems hardly credible that all this is represented by so small a population.

June 25. Having a most important engagement in London, which it was absolutely necessary for me to keep, I resolved upon returning there to-day, and therefore booked by way of Ostend for London.

The shortest sea-trip across the Channel is by way of Calais—Dover; but, as I had already been twice by this route, I preferred, by way of a change, to go *via* Ostend—Dover.

I left Brussels at about 8 a.m., reaching Ostend at 10 a.m., where, having gone on board the steamer, we reached Dover in four hours. The sea was calm, but a very strong thunderstorm had come on, and the rain came down in torrents, and it was not until we reached within a few minutes off Dover that this unpleasant weather ceased. During

June 26 *to July* 1, having attended to my engagements, I visited the Masonic School for Boys, at Wood Green, near London, at which two hundred and sixty-five boys are being educated, at the expense of Freemasons. This institution is ably managed by the enthusiastic Secretary, Mr. Bincks. I was told that this gentleman succeeded in raising no less than twenty-two thousand pounds for this charity. Here is again another instance of English charity : all these orphan children, who, perhaps, otherwise might be uncared for, are clothed, fed, and receive a decent education. It was a great pleasure to me to go through this institution.

I also took this opportunity of going to the Lyceum Theatre, where I heard the performance of "The Lyons Mail," by Mr. Henry Irving and Miss Terry; also Toole's Theatre, where I saw the famous Toole, in "Artful Cards" and "Namesakes"; and the St. James', where Mr. and Mrs. Kendall performed "Impulse."

I also visited the printing works of Messrs. Standidge and Co., Messrs. Elmore and Co , and Messrs. Francis and Co. I returned to Brussels by 8.40 a.m., *viâ* Dover, on

July 1. We re-crossed the Channel, per steamer "Marie Louise," and, after a very enjoyable trip, reached, at about 3 p.m., the pretty seaside town of Ostend. This is one of the most fashionable resorts on the seaside for the Continent; more especially that the town was in gala on this Sunday morning, I saw it to great advantage. Thousands of people were swarming on the beach, and the whole place was decorated with flags. Bands were playing on all sides, and there were all kinds of amusements for the pleasure seeking. I arrived the same evening at Brussels.

July 2. Visited the Musée de Peinture, being the celebrated picture gallery, containing some of the finest specimens of the old masters. One of the first pictures of note, Quentin Matsy's "Holy Family," was bought by the Museum from one of the churches for ten thousand pounds. This painting did not convey to one the grand feeling when viewing the lifelike expressions produced by Rubens or Rembrandt, for further on we see a picture by the former of "Worshipping by the Wise Men," which is a marvel of painting.

It would be impossible to name the wonderful pictures we see here worthy of note; for there are few that are not good, if any, and the quantity of pictures exhibited is very great.

Visited the Park, in the centre of the town and close to the Hotel de l'Europe, where we were staying. This is a very elegantly laid out park, with several ponds and fountains, and is the rendezvous of the upper ten of Brussels. In the evening we went to an open-air concert, what is called the "Wauxhall," but which really forms part of the park grounds. The band playing was that of the Opera House, and consisted of eighty-five well trained musicians. It was very pleasant in the cool of the evening to hear this concert, and also watch the fashionable world of Brussels, who were attracted here in large numbers.

July 3. Hardly any visitor to Brussels would omit visiting the battlefield of Waterloo. We took the train, therefore, this morning to Braine l'Alleud, which is the nearest spot for the centre of the battlefield. At the station a carriage met us, which conveyed us to the Hotel du Musée.

This hotel is kept by the niece of Serjeant-Major Cotton, one of the veterans under Wellington. On entering we were received by this lady, and shown a most wonderful collection of relics of the battle—guns, swords, bayonets, clothing and uniforms, coins, helmets, casques, etc., of English, French, Prussian, Dutch, and of other soldiers intermingled, beaten about, torn, and worn as only war can do it.

The most interesting relics are: the sword of General Macdonald, which he used during the battle, and which has a quantity of dents and breaks on its edges, showing how desperately it was used. A pair of spurs worn by Napoleon, made of silver, and some utensils of this General's kitchen; also a dragoon's saddle-bags, with the stains of blood still visible, are of interest.

We were also shown a quantity of bones and skulls, the bone of a soldier with two bullets in it, the skull of another with a sword-cut, and another with a bullet in the temple—a sad spectacle, especially when we can see that they were all young men, for there was none among them with a tooth missing.

We now leave the hotel, and mount the Monument of the Lion. This is a large earth mound, artificially made in pyramid shape, with two hundred and thirty-five steps to walk up; on the top of this, a huge lion is placed, weighing twenty-eight tons, and cast of the guns captured from the French. From the top of this we get an excellent view over the whole battlefield, and, with plan in hand and guide to indicate the names of the various villages and hills, we can follow the course. The spot where General Blucher met the Duke of Wellington is pointed out, and at this spot a small memorial is placed. At the foot of this memorial is the grave of General Gordon, Aide-de-Camp to the Duke of Wellington. The old guide I just spoke of told us that he lost his father at this battle.

We return to Brussels by train, and visit the "Galeries St. Hubert," an arcade built something after the style of the Burlington in London, with beautiful shops of all descriptions. We now turn our way to the Hotel de Ville. This is undoubtedly the most extraordinary building in Brussels, and one of the largest and most handsome buildings in Belgium. It was built in about the year 1402. The façade is in the Gothic style, and its peculiarly shaped spire is about four hundred feet high, but for some unknown reason was not placed in the centre of the building.

The interior of the building is used as the offices of the Municipality and the reception rooms I visited. They are very handsome, and have a great quantity of Flemish tapestry and paintings, mostly relating to the old worthies of Brussels. The grand saloon is very handsome, being decorated with carved wood in Gothic style, and is about one hundred feet long and eighty feet broad. In this saloon the British and other officers were dancing when they were suddenly called off to the field of Waterloo.

In going down we have a view of the Place de l'Hotel de Ville. This square is of very great interest, as most of the high buildings surrounding it were built at about the same date as the Hotel de Ville, and one can almost imagine himself among the inhabitants of Brussels five hundred years ago.

The chief edifices here of note are the halls or guilds. The carpenters, brewers, butchers, mariners, and rangers, are the most conspicuous. Some other new buildings are being erected by the Government here, and they are wisely carrying out the same architecture as the other buildings, so as not to interfere with the look of this interesting square.

Visited the statue of the Mannekin, which is considered one of the famous sights of this city.

We now go on to the Cathedral of St. Gudule. The outside of this building is not very attractive, but the interior is very beautiful, particularly the glass windows built between the years 1600 and 1700. A pulpit carved out of wood is a most marvellous piece of workmanship, and represents the Expulsion of Adam and Eve out of Paradise. The pulpit itself is carried by a tree, and all around animals of all descriptions are placed in an artistic manner; surrounding the whole is the image of the Virgin killing the serpent. It is almost incredible that the whole of this beautiful and large piece of work should have been done in carved wood.

In the evening we went to the Eden Theatre, which is built in exactly the same style as that in Paris. There were some ballets and a few other varied performances.

July 4. Visited a manufactory of Brussels lace. The patience these girls have who are making the lace by hand is beyond praise. They are seated with a large pillow in front of them full of a hundred or more of bobbins and the same quantity of pins, which they continually shift about alternately. Their work is so small and fine that, unless with the most careful attention and study, it is impossible to follow how it is done. A small piece that one of the women had before her, about two inches by three inches, took her a whole week to make!

Drove to the Column of Congress, which stands on one of the principal avenues and the highest part of the town. It was erected in memory of the Belgian

Constitution, and is about one hundred and forty feet high. It is a rather plain column, surmounted by the statue of Leopold I., King of the Belgians. At the four corners of the columns four lions are placed, above which stand allegorical figures of Justice, Freedom of Religion, the Press.

We drive along the beautiful boulevards and reach the Palace of Justice, which is still unfinished, and certainly seems an unnecessarily large and elaborate building. This is to contain the civil and criminal courts. It was supposed to cost two millions, but by the time it is complete the expense will be over three millions sterling. The inhabitants are very sore about this lavish expenditure, and the town in consequence has been heavily taxed. I witnessed a great demonstration of a few thousand people who were parading the streets in procession to protest against any more of the proposed taxes being made.

After a pretty drive through this town went to the Musée du Nord. This place contains a most varied set of amusements. After witnessing a small entertainment of singers, dancers, etc., we descend to the next floor, where, in a series of small halls, all kinds of amusements are provided. The Giant (Chinese) Chang, eight feet four inches tall, the beauty without a body, waxwork, shows, automatons, panoramas, etc., etc., were all on view. A hall for athletic sports, games, reading rooms, billiards—in fact, everything imaginable in the way of amusements, and the whole of this for one franc entrance fee. This certainly was, and I may say will be, the cheapest entertainment I have had or may be likely to expect.

The next morning,

July 5, we left Brussels for Antwerp. We first drive to the Docks. What a busy place this is! The famous port I have only been able to imagine up to the present, I have before me. A forest of masts of ships from all quarters of the globe. Here lie huge piles of jute, hemp, cotton, wool—side by side. There, for goodness knows what value, the piles and piles of wooden beams, logs, boards, and planks; over there mountains of boxes, bales, or petroleum barrels. I enjoyed the bustle and busy scene around me.

We visit the Cathedral after luncheon. A very handsome and noble structure, and of the same size, I think, as the Strasburg one, with a magnificent spire; the whole built in Gothic style.

The interior is very grandly finished work, and especially the carved wood. Altar and choir are in themselves worth a visit. Over the altar hangs one of the masterpieces of Rubens, representing the Transfiguration of the Virgin. This is a splendid work. The well-known group of angels is exquisite. The two other pictures painted by this wonderful artist are, it is needless to say, most strikingly beautiful.

We now go to the Picture Gallery, where we view

the excellent collection of the Flemish and Dutch school. The quantity of paintings bearing the names of Rubens, Vandyck, Teniers, etc., is quite enough guarantee that we see a number of good pictures, and it would be impossible, as I go from gallery to gallery, to ponder over the various productions that would attract special attention.

In going through this gallery, I must here mention that I witnessed one of the most extraordinary sights conceivable. As we find in all galleries students, male and female, copying pictures, so here; but what was my surprise when I saw one of them sitting on a low stool, with his easel before him and palette in hand— no, I should say foot, and brush in the other foot. On closer inspection it is noticed that the poor man has no arms, but his coat-sleeves are put into his side pockets, and the leisurely way in which he uses his feet is apt to deceive a passer-by, without noticing this peculiar man. He now takes up his palette in one foot, with as much ease as any person could do it with his hands, he takes up with the other his paint tube, carefully unscrews the small screw, and then presses out in the usual way the colour on the palette. The ease with which he does everything is quite astounding. The screwing and unscrewing of these tiny tops is quite ridiculously strange; in fact, his toes are used with as much ease as we might use our fingers. I spoke to him, and he spoke English very fairly. He said that he was born without arms, and had, consequently, to make the best use he could of his feet. In fact, he had brought this art of his to such perfection that his painting is very good indeed, and exact, and he uses his feet in such a steady manner that he even shaves himself!

We now go to the Church of St. Jacques. The exterior of this is very simple, in fact, it resembles a factory more than anything else; but on entering it we are surprised at the richness of its decorations. Most magnificent marble pillars reach to the very height of the interior of this rather lofty structure, one set of columns in black and white and another in red.

We now drive up the Boulevards, and pass the Flemish Theatre, which is a very handsome building indeed, and further on reach the Zoological Gardens. This is a very good collection, and, I am told, one of the best in Europe. The gardens are tastefully laid out, and the arrangements of the whole place were very good.

We now take the train to Rotterdam, and arrive there in a couple of hours. A carriage soon drives us up the Boomjees, or quay. In the river are lying alongside hundreds of boats of all kinds and dimensions, and the scene we have here is similar to that at Antwerp. The quay is a very long one, and is lined with limes (hence its name, meaning The Limes).

The town itself is very pleasing, and, considering

the busy state it is in, it is very clean. The streets are broad in the main thoroughfares, and the river Maas has four very good bridges thrown across it, especially one of them with six spans—a very handsome structure.

The whole town is, furthermore, intersected with a great number of canals. This is a very great advantage in so busy a place, as the traffic for loading and unloading the ships at the quay is mostly done by barges.

One of the prettiest little drives imaginable is that in the Park at Rotterdam. The gardens and lawns are so well kept that it was a great pleasure driving round them. After further driving round the town, and seeing the principal streets and buildings of the city, which are only peculiar as regards their construction in the old Dutch style, we get to the station, on our way to the Hague, which is reached at 10.30 p.m. We go to the Hotel Belle Vue, where we are now glad to get some rest.

July 6. We are up early, and after breakfast take a drive round this small but lovely town. What a difference here to Antwerp or Rotterdam. Here we are in a quiet town, away from all bustle. Every street is lined with trees, and, looking over the Hague, we might call it a large park, covered with beautiful villas and small mansions. The cleanliness of the Dutch is here to be observed in particular. The servants seem to be scrubbing their doors and windows all the day, and even their streets and pavements are cleaner than I have seen them anywhere else. No wonder that the King of the Netherlands has chosen this lovely place for his residence.

There is a small steam tramway line from the Hague to Scheveningen. I take advantage of riding for the first time in this sort of conveyance, and after a drive of twenty minutes, which all the way is along a handsome avenue of limes, arrive close to the beach of this famous seaside resort. This is said to be the most fashionable on the Continent.

The beach was crowded with people, and the view, on approaching it, was very beautiful. A hundred or two of people were there playing, chatting, and no doubt flirting in the basket chairs which are strewed by hundreds on the beach. Opposite us are stationed, in rows, numbers of bathing machines, on the one side for gentlemen, and on the other for ladies; these are continually conveying their burdens backwards and forwards at short distances apart. Booths are erected on the beach, in which you can purchase any seaside requisites. The usual donkeys for a ride through the sands are also to be hired here.

Very handsome and spacious hotels line the beach; one of them, especially, is kept by the Government. The whole town contains, in reality, nothing but hotels and shops, as otherwise it is only a small fishing hamlet. A very handsome arcade, with excellent shops, forms one of the promenades in the town.

I return again by this handsome and shaded avenue of trees to the Hague. Here a carriage is hired for a drive in the park, which is very extensive, and forms a magnificent plantation of oaks and beeches, full of round ornamental lakes and islands, very tastefully arranged. This is one of our best drives, so far. By payment of a fee, we enter the "Palace in the Wood," or, as the Dutch style it, "Bosch" (Bush). The apartments are very nice indeed; but the only one worth special notice is the Chinese Saloon, furnished with presents from the Emperor of China. The tapestry, in silk needlework, is very exquisite; the various wood cabinets are also very handsome. We visit the various monuments; the one requiring special attention is that of the Nation, called the Memorial of 1813, in memory of the first Constitution.

We leave this beautiful town in the afternoon for Amsterdam, and after a ride across a very flat country, we reach Amsterdam late in the evening, where we put up at the Hotel Doelin ("Doelin": Bull's-eye).

July 7. Amsterdam is built on piles driven into peat and sand to a depth of about sixty feet, and is protected from the sea by dykes on the Y or Ij. The whole city is crossed by canals, and forms ninety-five islands. Its streets although well-kept, are narrow and crooked, and the buildings, on the whole, are not handsome. Most of them are built in the old Dutch style, and form a great contrast to the more recently erected structures. The principal attraction here is the International Exhibition. On arriving at the station one could already see the town must be full. The trains were packed, and when we arrived at the hotel we found there also a great crush.

The first thing, of course, is to take a cab to the Exhibition, which is duly done, and we arrive at the grand entrance, which gives one a very good impression on entering. It is formed of two huge pyramids, about one hundred and fifty yards apart, carried by four huge elephants, surmounted with a peculiar combination of statues, busts, trees, fruits, wild animals, and snakes, the elephants forming the base, and the others the cone of the pyramids. Across these two structures an imitation of Indian shawl pattern is tastefully imitated, and the whole is, I think, meant to represent the Indian possessions of the Dutch.

The Exhibition, it must be said, is a private enterprise, and not as successful as it might be, more particularly that it is still in an unfinished state, although it was opened in May. In fact, many people seem to think it will be closed before it is completed. Still, due credit must be given to what there is here. The grand entrance, of course, leads to the Dutch departments, out of which branch off the various foreign expositions.

The show cases are fitted up with their various products in very tasteful style, and it is only under a general head that so large an enterprise can be in any way described. The foreign countries exhibiting and requiring special notice are the Belgians, Russians, and Chinese; other countries, of course, from every part of the globe, had their space allotted them, and have filled it, for England, America, Austria, Germany, Spain, France, etc., etc., are all here, but not so prominent as the three countries I specially observed.

The Belgian machinery and iron department was very good indeed, and does credit to the busy little kingdom.

Here were the Chinamen, pigtail and all, with their exquisite Chinese vases and woodwork, and in particular, the quantity and choice of their exhibits require special note.

The Russian furs and products are well displayed, and form a variety to the monotonous show cases of say, candles, tobacco, matches, hemp, cotton, cloth, etc., etc., represented by every country, and their excellence only to be observed by the keen eye of a juryman or a connoisseur.

The Dutch have made a very great effort to show off their colonies, and I think with success.

A troupe of Javanese was a very interesting

feature of their exhibits. We enter a small enclosure upon which are erected the huts of this peculiar people, built of bamboo, and covered with palm leaves, etc. In the centre, a band of musicians and dancers are performing; they play on copper drums, which look more like saucepans and kettles, and are all squatted on the ground, about fifteen or twenty in number, each one with two rows of drums before him, which he strikes with a wooden hammer. The tones produced are rather mellow, but the tunes are very peculiar. The conductor of the band, who plays on the largest assortment of drums, starts the first few notes, and the others follow. There is among them one stringed instrument, about the size of an ordinary fiddle; also a triangle and castanettes. This band is seated in a circle, and in the centre two women are dancing. They are dressed in loose garments of coloured silk, and are covered with bracelets, nose-rings, and other native jewellery. Their skin is dark, and they are, compared with the rather ugly, bony-faced men, rather good looking. Their dancing, as they call it, is very curious, for it forms really only a series of posing in what they must think graceful positions. Their movements are so slow that they are hardly perceptible.

Another exhibition is the South American Indians and the Creoles. They are supposed to be in their own villages, and show the kind of life in their own country. Their costumes are most peculiar, and varied, and some are dressed like the North American Indians, with coloured feathers in their heads and on their legs; others have peculiar turbans for head-dress, and are tattooed in all kinds of ways. They have with them their wives and daughters, who are also clothed in their different peculiar costumes.

The gardens of the Exhibition contain various restaurants of different nations. Also numerous other kinds of special industries, the most interesting being the diamond splitting and polishing. We had lunch at the English restaurant, and then visited the various Colonial exhibitions.

On entering the Indian Department I was rather disappointed to find it so poorly represented. We first saw a row of Bengal shops, with a figure of some kind of salesman or woman in each, selling fish, grain, fruit, etc.; this was an exhibit of the Government of Bengal. Calcutta showed its fine teas, and Midnapore Jail exhibited various descriptions of coir rugs, carpets, etc.

From the Bombay side there was little of importance, except some Indian jewellery by Watson & Co., of Bombay.

South Australia, New Zealand, and Ceylon were also represented.

The Bavarian, Hungarian, Swiss, and other countries were shown at small chalets and other structures.

arranged as refreshment bars, in which one is served by girls dressed in their own national costumes,

July 8. We visit the Zoological Gardens close to the Park, which is one of the best collections in Europe. The arrangements here are very excellent. The most interesting was the ourang outang, the first specimen I have seen. He had a very nice place to himself, with a chair and table, also a bed; his movements were certainly something like that of a funny little old man. The lions, giraffes, lamas, and musk deer were specially good specimens.

After a couple of hours in the Zoo, we drove through the town, and visited the various places of interest and the Botanical Gardens.

We take the train in the evening for Hanover. This is one of the most disagreeable rides possible. Almost the whole of the way is a sandy plain, and the windows of our carriage have to be kept shut, in consequence of the fearful amount of dust. We got a little sleep, and arrive at 3 a.m. in Hanover.

July 9. This town should be of some interest to Englishmen, for it was held by British sovereigns for more than a hundred years, and as recently as 1837, when it was given over to its own government; was governed by a King until 1866, when it was annexed by Prussia, and made one of its Provinces, after the war with Austria. We stay at the Hotel de Russie, a very good and comfortable hotel, which we appreciate all the more after the great crush at the Doelin in Amsterdam. The old part of the town which we drive to is well worth a visit. The quaint old houses, three and four hundred years old, built in the peculiar old German style, are very interesting. Amongst the new structures are, firstly, the Railway Station, which is the handsomest I have yet seen. In fact, the only remark one must make against it is that it is by far too large and elaborate for a town containing only a hundred and fifty thousand inhabitants. The Post-office is also a very fine edifice.

Hanover is a military station, and one is compelled to observe the extraordinary military discipline throughout. The railway officials, down to the guards and porters, as well as the post-office officials, are all soldiers, and they seem more as if they were on parade at their work, instead of business.

July 10. We take a drive round the palace and grounds, and also pay a visit to the well-known stables containing the special white breed of horses. This is a beautiful breed which is kept up at the expense of the State. The breed is a cross of Arab and European blood, and this has been so carefully kept, that there is not one spec of any colour but white to be seen on the whole animal. The coat, hoofs, mouth, nostrils, and even eyes, are perfectly white. The total number of horses kept are one hundred and twenty-five, and as they increase they are sold off; but, of course, it is not one in ten or fifteen foals that is suitable to keep for the collection; for if one of them has the slightest defect, that is, any colour about it, it is at once discarded.

We also inspected the old State carriages and harness. These are very fine; but the chief interest is historical, as they all bear the English arms, the first King of Hanover having been the Duke of Cumberland.

Before leaving Hanover, I must say that I had the pleasure of meeting, at the Hotel de Russie, Mr. I. S. Bergheim, the eldest brother of my friend. About 5 p.m. we leave Hanover for Hamburgh, reaching there at 9 p.m.

July 11. We are staying at the Hotel de l'Europe, facing the Elbe, and from our window command an excellent view of the river, which, especially at night, is very fine.

This morning we visit the harbour and quays. The former is very long, and extends down the banks of the Elbe, about four miles in length. This river is connected with a number of canals running into the town, and therefore makes it very convenient for the transport of goods as unloaded from these vessels. The quays, four in number, are very conveniently built. They are each three thousand yards in length, and one hundred broad. Extensive buildings are erected on each side of them, to facilitate the loading and unloading. About sixty steamers can be accommodated on each side. The cargoes are discharged by moveable cranes, running along the sides of the quays. The third quay is the largest, and here is the pier of the Trans-Atlantic Steamship Company. We visited (on payment of a small fee to the Seaman's Asylum) one of the steamers, called the "Westphalia," a very fine steamer (2500 tons).

The city is very well built, with good streets and a great deal of water communication. The Jungferstieg is the principal street, and contains some very massive structures. We visit St. Nicholas Cathedral, a new structure, built after the plan of Sir Gilbert Scott. The steeple is about four hundred and fifty feet high, and is designed after the Cologne one. The interior is richly decorated with marble, and the vestry door, of wood, with inlaid mother-o'-pearl, made by a Hamburg gentleman, is very handsome, and of extraordinary accurate workmanship. We were told it was made by one of two brothers, the second giving it to the church as a present. It took twenty-one years to make.

We visited the interior of the Exchange, which was a very busy place, and seemed too small for the purpose; but on going out, we noticed they were making extensive additions.

Visited the various Memorials, the most important being "Kriegersdeukneal" (Warrior's Monument), erected in memory of the Franco-German War. This was a small one, but nevertheless very impressive indeed. It represented two dying soldiers being crowned with victory and honour; at their side a fallen and a dying horse. The whole group is only slightly over life-size, and stands on a small granite pedestal, with a piece of garden around it. The pedestal bears the names of the citizens of Hamburg who fell during the war.

We now drive to the Agricultural Show, where we see an excellent exhibition of horses, cows, oxen, pigs, sheep, etc. The English, as regards horses, are of course at the top of the tree; they exhibited eighteen horses, and took sixteen prizes and the two grand medals. The sheep were very fine, and the pigs enormous; one of them weighed 630 lbs. Agricultural implements, etc., were also exhibited, and, on the whole, this show was well worth a visit.

We now go to the station to take the train to Berlin, and, fortunately enough, we were very early for our train, otherwise we should have had the pleasure of missing it. The town of Hamburg is one of the free towns of Germany, and therefore has its own Customs; but instead of examining luggage on entering, it is done on leaving the place. So that on our arrival at the station we were huddled into an inspecting room, and, as the Cattle Show was on, it can be readily imagined that there was a great crowd there; also the quality need not be defined. We had to wait until our turn came, and it was quite amusing to see the officers inspecting everything, and pulling out the smallest new article to charge duty on it. One poor man had bought a few yards of print, no doubt for his wife or daughter. There certainly was not more than ten yards of it; he was charged duty, and had to pay seven pfennigs, about one half-penny, for which he duly got a receipt!

Curiously enough, nothing of ours was opened. I suppose it was our good looks that led to this phenomenon!

We get into the carriage, made ourselves comfortable, and arrive in Berlin the following morning at about seven o'clock.

July 12. We stay at the Hotel d'Angleterre. After having made ourselves comfortable, we now go about to view the great city of the German Empire. I did not expect to find Berlin, in general, so fine a place as it turned out to be. The principal street close to our hotel, " Unter den Linden " (under the Limes), is a very noble thoroughfare, having a fine avenue of limes running through its centre. We first pass the monument of Frederick the Great, upon a pedestal of granite, surrounded with bronze groups of his generals, and upon the top the King on horseback ; opposite is the palace of the Emperor of Germany. Opposite the further end of the street is the Brandenburgher Thor, a gate with five passages of rather clumsy structure.

and having on the top the Chariot of Victory. The only interest attached to this gate is that the Statue of Victory was carried away by the French to Paris, and, after the Battle of Waterloo, was brought back again by the Prussians. Passing the gate, we came to the Park, the chief feature here being the Siegessanté (Column of Victory); this was erected after the Franco-German War, but is also intended to be a memorial of the Wars of 1864 and 1866. It is a large, high column, standing on a pedestal of granite, forming a sort of hall, which is called the Victory Hall, adorned with mosaic pictures relating to the subject. On the column, built of sandstone, are placed, at various intervals, the cannons captured from the French and the Austrians. The monument, it may be said, is not liked by the Germans, in consequence of the column representing victories won by the Prussians alone against the Austrians, when, as it is well known, they fought and defeated the Hanoverians, who had joined the Austrians; the former more especially having fought for the Germans so well in 1870 and 1871. The whole column is surmounted by a gilt Statue of Victory, thirty-two feet in height.

The University, the Royal Castle, and the Palace of the Crown Prince, are all in the vicinity, and are very handsome structures.

July 13. In the morning we went for a walk through the beautiful Arcade, Unter den Linden, and visited the Paroplicum. This is a very elaborate wax-work exhibition. The usual kind of things, as the sleeping beauty, the dying soldiers, etc., etc., are to be seen here, and are well made. The most interesting group was that of the Berlin Congress, where we could see the divers statesmen sitting in the proper positions they occupied during the Congress here, and, as far as I could judge, were all good likenesses.

A very large collection of other amusing and interesting groups, etc., were to be seen.

We now spend the rest of the day in viewing the large Museum, Picture Gallery, and National Gallery. These are magnificent collections of science and art.

July 14. To-day we visit Potsdam. We take the train, it is about half an hour's ride, and arrive at one of the loveliest spots conceivable. The whole of Potsdam is one big garden, with villas peeping between the trees here and there.

We take a drive towards the Palace, and every minute are more and more delighted with the beautiful scenery. We reach, after about half an hour's drive, the Palace or Chateau of the Emperor, at Babelsberg. We are informed that in the absence of the Empress, visitors are allowed to view the Castle. We go up a flight of stairs and view the private rooms of the Empress. The bed-rooms, dressing, bath, and other rooms first, which are very sumptuously furnished; also the one on the other side, the drawing and reception rooms. We then go up another flight, and are shown into the room of the Emperor. What wonderful simplicity this venerable man lives in. Who would believe that the room we are now in is the study of so great a man. The small quantity of furniture is of the plainest description, but how much more curious is it on entering his bed-room to find what simplicity reigns here. All the furniture is of plain, varnished wood; in the centre is a plain oak table, a few chairs and ornaments, a few pictures, and lastly, the bed, are the whole contents of the room. The bed is narrow, and very small, and it is almost hard to believe that the Emperor should sleep in so small and simple a thing.

As we go down by another staircase we are shown the stick the Emperor is in the habit of using. It is a plain stick which he cut forty-five years ago, and the top is quite worn away with handling. The Emperor is now eighty-six years old. From here we drive through a beautiful set of parks, wood, gardens laid out with water-works, etc., in lovely style, and passing the Palace of Sans Souci, we visit the new Palace of the Crown Prince. This formed part of that occupied formerly by Frederick the Great. As the Prince is now staying here, we are not permitted to view the whole of it, but go through the library, the music and dancing saloons, very elaborately decorated, and finally, the Muschelsal, or the Saloon of Shells. This room was designed by Frederick the Great himself. It is a very spacious saloon, the walls and ceilings being decorated with shells, precious stones, minerals, etc. The ceiling is of most elaborate design, and is all made of shells of divers shapes and sizes. The columns supporting the building are decorated with rough rock crystals, malachite, bloodstones, etc., etc., but the whole of the saloon is covered with stones and shells. We return from this beautiful place to Berlin by the evening train.

July 15. We leave this morning for Dresden, which we reach in the afternoon. We go to Weber's Hotel, and on looking out of the window notice that a tremendous crowd had collected, and that the town was decorated with flags, etc.; on enquiry, we find that a feast of the soldiers who fought in 1870-71, is going on. The Saxon troops had arranged to meet here for three days, and according to their programme, had to pass in procession through the town. This we did not fail to witness. A very long procession of about two thousand men passed us, carrying banners of their trades and guilds, with their brass bands, some on horseback, others in carriages, and on foot. The procession closed with a couple of carts, containing what was supposed to be French prisoners of war, in their uniforms, and lastly, a chariot drawn by six horses, containing a young woman representing

Germania, with drawn sword and shield, and around her four young girls, supposed to represent the four rivers of Germany.

We now go to the Belvedere Terrace. This is a large promenade built on the highest point of Dresden, from which we can overlook the town and the river Elbe. The view is very good, and under the shady trees of the Belvedere restaurant we can enjoy the beautiful cool air, together with the music of a first-class band, and the sight of the *beau monde* of Dresden, who flock here every evening.

We now go to the Opera, the piece being the "Barbier de Seville." What a magnificent house! This is the most beautiful one I have seen as yet. The Opera House in London is not nearly so fine; it may be somewhat larger, but certainly not so well arranged or decorated. This comic opera is very amusing, and the music pleasing. The principal singer, Fraulien von Weber, has a beautiful voice. I must say I was quite astonished to find in so small a town so splendid a building and so excellent a performance.

July 16. We make our way early to the Picture Gallery. This is one of the most renowned picture galleries in the world, in which the works of some of the best of the old masters are exhibited. In going through this magnificent collection, one could not help asking how could this little kingdom have managed to collect these wonderful treasures. Is it possible to go into details of the grand pictures of Rubens, painted by him when at the height of his excellence, or into the grandeur of conception, the well-ordered composition, or the examples of power of the Flemish and Italian schools?

One picture I must mention, and that is the world-renowned picture of Raphael's Madonna (San Sisto). It is described, "The Virgin Mary, with the Infant in her arms, borne up by clouds; on her right, St. Sixtus in a kneeling posture; on her left, St. Barbara; below, two cherubs; and in the background, between two curtains, a halo of angelic heads." Both in tone and feeling, this picture is a marvel of workmanship and conception. We feel at once, on looking at it, a life-like reality of the group, and the more we look at it, the more is this impression deepened and the figures show something new to us. It is one of those productions over which one might spend hours in admiring. We leave these beautiful collections, and enter the Museum Place, which is a square of magnificent buildings, and take a drive through the town. Two very handsome bridges across the Elbe are well worth notice.

We leave Dresden in the afternoon, *en route* for Prague, and shortly reach the German frontier, where after passing the plain of the Elbe valley, we come upon the picturesque Saxon Switzerland. The valley is narrow and rocky, and the railway occasionally hewn through the solid rock. One of the finest points here is the Konigstein, rising about eight hundred feet above the river, and commanding a noble prospect. At Bodenbach, the frontier, we are received by the Austrian officials, after the inspection of our luggage, and in a few minutes we are in Bohemia.

All the way to Prague we traverse lovely scenery; also the various battle-fields, where the Turks were beaten at Raudnitz, the Austrians beaten by the Prussians at Lobositz. We reach Prague in the evening, and sleep at the Hotel Schwarzes Ross.

July 17. This ancient capital of Bohemia is chiefly interesting from a historical point of view. The position it occupies is strikingly picturesque and imposing. It lies in the valley of the Moldau, across which two handsome bridges are to be seen: the one very old, with sixteen spans, and about six hundred yards long—this is called the Carlsbüche; the other is a suspension bridge, also about the same length, and with the monument of Francis I. This memorial, at the same time, serves as a handsome fountain. Still further on are two more bridges.

In driving now through the town, its quaint, old-fashioned Bohemian buildings are rather interesting, such as the old University building, which is about five hundred years old, most of which has, however, now been renovated. This University is one of the first of the Austrian Empire.

The Palace of Wallenstein (1623), the famous general of the Thirty Years' War, is also of interest.

We now take the train for Vienna, passing *via* Pardubitz, Bohmisch, Trübau, Brunn, and Gäuserdorf. As we are swiftly traversing this lovely and peaceful-looking country, the whole of which consists of a line of beautifully wooded hills, fertile and picturesque valleys, covered with seemingly thriving villages and towns, it seems hard to believe that the whole of this was the site of many battles.

The Hussite Wars terminated here in 1434. The Hungarians fought here in 1260 and 1278. Frederick the Great was beaten by the Austrians in 1757. The Swedes were also here in the sixteenth century. The battlefields of Wagram and Austerlitz are also not far from us; and the battles of 1854 and 1866 help to increase the historical interest connected with this district. We are served in the train with a first-rate luncheon, ordered for us by our polite Austrian guard.

It is really necessary to lay stress on the politeness of the Austrians in general. The French are supposed to excel in this respect, and although we met through the whole of our journey really nothing but the greatest politeness, still, I think the Austrians must have the preference. We arrive at Vienna in the evening. Hotel Kaiserin Elisabeth.

July 18. As the most important edifice of Vienna is the Church of St. Stephen, we, of course, visit that first. It is about five hundred years old, built of limestone, in the shape of a cross, and is very richly built in the Gothic style. It has two towers, one unfinished, and the other four hundred and fifty three feet high. The interior is very grand, and contains some very handsome carved choir stalls.

The Sarcophagus of Frederick III. is a very elaborate work in red and white marble, and stands in one of the wings.

We now visit the famous Vienna Picture Gallery, as well as all other galleries, of which it is not possible to give a description in detail; but suffice it to say, that they are all most excellent collections, and we were well rewarded by an inspection of them. In the evening we visited the Opera House, and heard "Mignon," by Ambroise Thomas.

This is an edifice which does credit to the Austrian nation. On entering, one is at once struck with the splendid arrangements of entrance and exit. The theatre itself is surrounded with very wide corridors, having, at short distances apart, large folding doors. The boxes, upper boxes, and galleries have also each three large and separate exits, so that in case of need, the whole house could be cleared with the greatest ease in no time. The decoration of the interior is sumptuous, and the place will seat comfortably three thousand persons. It would be absurd to compare this grand structure to either Her Majesty's or Covent Garden in London, and it is extraordinary that the great city of London should be so far behind foreigners in this respect. Surely, if any nation can afford to spend money on such buildings, it ought to be the English first. "Mignon" was very well produced, and the orchestra especially was excellent.

July 19 and 20. Having made an appointment with the photographer, I go there first thing in the morning; and, after the usual tortures, we are off again sight seeing.

The streets of this capital are very elegant, and we pass, one after another, huge blocks of magnificent buildings. The Ring Strasse encircles the entire inner part of the city; it is about fifty yards wide, and over two miles in length. The handsomeness of its architecture is undoubtedly unsurpassed in any other European capital.

The Schotten and Franzensring, forming part of the Ring Strasse, are the most magnificent parts of Vienna. A large number of new and elaborate buildings have been here constructed, amongst others the one still under completion is the Ring Theatre, which is being rebuilt.

The enormous University, the new Rathhaus, built in Italian palatial style, lavishly adorned with statues; the Palace of Justice in German style, and the magnificent Imperial Opera House are a set of buildings in this street at which we can only gaze in bewildering surprise. Nothing but palatial residences and elegant government structures are to be seen all through the whole of this long and well laid out street. At another part of the Ring Strasse is the Burgring, containing the rich Museum, lavishly constructed in Renaissance style, with a profusion of statues, and on the dome two colossal statues of Helios and Athena. Opposite is a beautiful park.

The river Danube itself does not flow through the town, but the town is divided by the Wien and the Danube canal, over which a number of bridges lead to the outer town. The Elisabeth bridge is the handsomest.

The manners and customs of the Viennese are slightly different from those of their neighbours. Their streets are perfectly empty and dark at half-past ten. Their hotels are really only furnished rooms, for they do not provide table d'hôte ; the visitor must go to the restaurant for it. We dined and lunched at various places, amongst them the best being Sachse's restaurant, a first-rate place, where we had an excellent dinner. The cafés also vary slightly from those elsewhere, and they are very good indeed. Ices are consumed in large quantities here, and the varieties are very curious ; their quality is also better than in any other part of Europe.

Before leaving Vienna, I must not omit to mention the Grabon (ditch or moat). This street was formerly a moat of the old fortifications, and is now lined with very attractive shops, and although not a long one, is still the principal business street in Vienna.

July 21. We leave this morning at 6.30 p.m. for Lintz, by boat. We start off through the canal in a small vessel, and are shortly in the Danube, where we change to a handsome river steamer.

The weather is very fine indeed, and we have every prospect of a beautiful trip. For some time the river is not very attractive, but in an hour or two the scenery gradually gets much better. An extensive and wealthy abbey forms a centre of attraction. It is an enormous structure, and its high position on the hill is very good. Further on, we come to a number of very picturesquely situated villages, with their ruined abbeys and towers, and as we go on we are more and more delighted with the view before us. The greenly-clad mountains tower on either side of the river, and now and then a rock projects far into the stream. We are all the way passing small islands, which add to the beauty of the scenery. The shining sun on the tops of the mountains, many of them crowned with ruins of old castles or robbers' strongholds, and the valley, in the shade, with its black-looking fir trees, are sights never to be forgotten, but very hard to describe.

At Grein we reach what are called the "Strudel" (turbulent or gurgling water). The ridges of rock here again reach far into the stream, and this obstacle is surrounded by these rapids. The vessel labours hard against the rushing waters, and it takes four men to work the rudder. These rapids were at one time very dangerous, but the rocks were blasted, and the passage is now safe.

Near the village of Strudel, on the left bank, rises the ruin of the robber stronghold, Werferstern, and again an enormous rock, surmounted by a ruined tower, forms a new obstacle to the stream as it descends from the Strudel. The eddy thus caused constitutes the once dangerous whirlpool, which is now only a swift rapid. The passage of the Strudel and whirlpools only occupies a few minutes.

On and on we steam through the most charming and impressive scenery; the wild-looking rocky mountains contrasting with the fruitful valley below. Our journey occupied about eighteen hours, so that we saw the Danube in the morning, noon, and night. The sunset over the dark mountains was a grand sight, and never to be forgotten is the grandeur of the scenery by moonlight. It is now past one a.m. as we go under a suspension bridge close to Linz, and in a few minutes we are off the boat, and make for the nearest hotel (Erzherog Carl), where we are glad to get rest.

July 22. The next move is to take the train for Munich, *viâ* Salzburg. The scenery to the latter town is very pretty, but between that and Munich it is well worth notice. The line from Salzburg skirts thickly-wooded and grassy hills, beyond which town the Eastern Alps, and close to the line runs the rapid Salzach. The whole of this ride is simply delightful, and the names of two stations, Vogelesung and Rosenhein (song of the bird and home of roses) are very appropriate. We arrive at Munich in the evening, and stay at the Rheinischer Hof.

July 23. Munich has always been and still maintains its position as the leading school of painting, and one may also safely say, under the reign of the present king especially, that of music.

We had the good fortune of arriving here just as an International Art Exhibition was going on, and we, therefore, did not fail to pay that a visit. We were well repaid for our trouble, and it was really a very grand exhibition.

In driving through the town we view the colossal statue, in a sitting posture, of King Max Joseph, which is situated in the centre of the city, and faces the palace, a very large building.

We go on to the Siegesthor, or Gate of Victory, which is an imitation of the Triumphal Gate at Rome, and is surmounted by "Bavaria," drawn by lions. This fine structure forms an appropriate termination of the Ludwig Strasse, a very handsome street. Visit the "Bavaria" and Hall of Fame. The colossal statue of Bavaria, in bronze, measures seventy feet to the top of the wreath which the standing figure holds aloft in its hand. We ascend inside this enormous figure by a spiral staircase, and after about sixty steps, take a comfortable seat inside the head! from whence, through apertures, we have a very good view of the city. The Hall of Fame surrounds this colossus, and contains the busts of eighty Bavarian notabilities.

After visiting the various points of interest, also the Botanical Gardens, where we saw a quantity of extraordinary plants, we took a drive to the "English Garden," an enormous park of six hundred acres in extent. The Isur, which flows through Munich, provides this park with a lake, and the fine old trees are watered by the same river. As regards Munich itself, it must be said that, like most other German towns that I have seen, it is well kept, and the German military discipline is to be noticed everywhere. The streets are very good and wide, especially the Ludwig and the Maximilian Strasse. As to the buildings in general, they are handsome and well-built.

In the evening we went to a variety concert, which was very amusing; an exhibition of performing pigeons was very interesting. Munich is well known as the great beer-producing and, more especially, consuming town. It is quite remarkable to notice the quantities of breweries here; but when we are told that over twenty-eight millions of gallons are brewed yearly, of which four-fifths is consumed by a population of about two hundred and thirty thousand, we are no more surprised to think that all of them must be paying concerns.

July 24. We take the train this morning for Botzen, *viâ* Innsbruck, and go on the same line again up to Rosenheim; from there we branch off along the beautiful Inn Valley, continually crossing and re-crossing this stream, as the railway line runs close to the sides of the mountains above us. We reach Innsbruck, after having passed the fortress "Kufstein," which forms the Austrian frontier on the line. Here we are now in the beautiful Tyrol. As the view on this line is very fine, the Austrians, with their usual kindness, place an observation car at the back of the train. This is a large square compartment, large enough to seat about fifteen to twenty persons, and fitted on its three sides with large plate-glass windows. From here we can get a view of the mountains around, and watch the train gradually working its way up the mountain, until it is over the Brenner Pass, a very great height above the sea level. Now we begin to see the snowy peaks again. It is beautiful and almost incredible to look into the valley beneath, and see the railway line that we had come over far in the depths below.

Every now and then the passengers will rush to one or another side of the car to view the marvellous scenery. Far beneath us runs a rushing tributary of the Inn, and every now and then, on the right or left, a waterfall. Time passed very well in this train, and at 7.30 p.m. we reached Botzen, where we stayed overnight at the Kaiserkrone (Imperial Crown) Hotel. After dinner we took a walk round this quaint little Tyrolese town, and ordered our carriage to be ready to start early for our expedition over the Stelvio Pass.

July 25. We are now comfortably seated in a good open carriage, with our Tyrolese coachman driving a good pair of horses, and our luggage well strapped-up at the back. During the night we had a very heavy fall of rain; but we start, with our usual good fortune, in clear and beautiful weather. The morning air is very cool, and makes the journey quite delightful; more especially that we are now running along the fruitful and fertile valley of the Etoch. The whole of the road is lined with well-kept orchards, stocked with fruit trees, apples, pears, peaches, cherries, walnuts, plums, etc., etc.; the hills above are covered with vines. The peasants here are very industrious, for we cannot find the smallest patch of land along the whole of this valley which is not well-cultivated. The road itself is a most excellent one, and runs backwards and forwards across the Etoch, keeping on a level until we reach the large village of Meran, about four and a half hours' drive from Botzen. Here we rest our horses, and, after having partaken of some luncheon, are on our road again to Spondinig, being now in the Vintschgau, or the vine-lands of the Tyrol. The extraordinary cultivation around us, and also on the mountains above, is a very pleasant spectacle. We see houses and orchards on the tops of the mountains, and after passing many a picturesque village of these happy-looking people, we reach, in the evening, about half-past seven, the wayside inn of Spondinig, having broken our journey at Schlanders, where horses were rested, and we refreshed ourselves with some excellent milk. After dinner at the inn, or, rather, "New Hotel," as they call it, we were early in bed, and ready again at six a.m.,

July 26, to start. The whole day is occupied in ascending the mountain forming the Stelvio Pass. Before us we see already the snowy peaks of the Geisterspitze and Tucketspitze, and, after having ascended for an hour, the Madatch Glacier is distinctly visible. The excellent road leads on and on up the sides of the mountains. We cross the river by a long bridge, and reach Prad, which lies at the foot of the Stelvio route. The valley here becomes very narrow, and barely affords room for the road and the river, the latter rushing down the steep valley, and also forming many picturesque falls. Here lies the village of Stelvio, which gives the name to this route; and from this the road becomes more steep, and by the time we have done about five thousand feet above sea level, the village of Tarfor is reached. Before us we have a most beautiful view. The broad snowy pyramid of the Weisskugel towers in the background, and close before us stands the Madatchsfritze, with its beautiful glacier, the whole covered with snow; and above us, on our right, about two thousand feet higher, the road station of Franzenshöhe, which we are to reach in the course of two or three hours. On this road, now about two miles from Franzenshöhe, the spot is indicated to us by the coachman where the notorious murderer Tourville threw down his wife into the precipice beneath. It will be remembered that this man was tried by the Austrians, and acquitted on the ground that his wife had fallen down by accident. The unfortunate lady, however, being English, the British authorities were not satisfied with the verdict, and, upon his arrival in England, he was arrested and conveyed to Austria, where the matter was tried again, and it was distinctly proved against him that it was impossible for her to have fallen down at that spot. He was eventually found guilty and condemned to twenty years' imprisonment. We stepped out of the carriage and inspected the spot; and, on the face of it, it was evident that she could not have fallen down the precipice, as the slope is much too gradual, and is covered with stumps of large trees, which must have stopped the body from rolling down some fifteen hundred to two thousand feet below. The spot is indicated by a small cross, stating that here the accident occurred to the wife of Tourville, July 16th, 1876.

July 26. At Franzenshöhe we have luncheon, and after resting the horses for a couple of hours, we are on our way again, ascending in long windings the enormous slope above us. The grandeur of the view from the whole of this road is beyond description; on our left, and seemingly very close to us, the snow-covered peaks which I have mentioned become more visible, until at last we can see the whole set of mountains, about twelve thousand feet high, completely covered with snow, which are now glistening with the bright sun shining on them. As we are nearing the summit of the Stelvio Pass, the view becomes more grand; the whole range of mountains before us is one mass of glistening snow. It is gradually getting cooler as we ascend, and we ourselves are having the snow at our side. We have to take out our wraps, and very soon find ourselves surrounded with snow many feet deep, as if in a Russian winter, while in the valley visible below, the sun is burning hot. This is a most magnificent sight. We now have arrived at Ferdinandshöhe, the highest point being nine thousand and forty-five feet above sea level. This is the highest pass traversed by a carriage road. A column on this height marks the boundary of (Tyrol) Austria and Italy. A moment later we bid adieu to the Austrians, and now begin descending the heights, which it has taken us about twelve hours to climb. We shortly meet the custom-house officials, who politely enquire whether we have anything to declare, and upon our reply in the negative, pass our luggage without examination. We now begin to make a fair descent of the mountain, and the horses we have are going splendidly. The road, of course, descends again in curves into the valley of Bormio, which, from the top only, presents the aspect of a bleak valley, and surrounded by barren and wild-looking mountains almost destitute of any kind of vegetation. The Adda emerges from between these mountains, and rushes wildly into the valley below, forming at various intervals pretty cascades and picturesque waterfalls. The winding road is built on a succession of galleries in the rock, and every now and again we have to pass through a tunnel hewn out of the solid rock. After passing eight such tunnels and driving at a high speed for about two and three-quarter hours, we finally reach the hotel at Bormio, and are well ready for our dinner, which we very soon get.

The hotel is called the New Bath Hotel, a handsome building, situated on a high level, about four thousand five hundred feet, and is very much frequented in consequence of the mineral baths. The establishment is a very good one, and affords a fine view of the valley of Bormio and the surrounding mountains; it lies in a park, and is, indeed, a very nice place to stay at for a rest.

July 27. We are this morning again on the high road. Letting alone the wonderful and imposing scenery we traversed yesterday, a word must be said in praise of the Austrian Government who made this road, and keep it up in such a marvellous condition. No carriage road in any part of the world could be found that is kept in a better condition, and the engineering skill displayed is itself an object of interest.

A fresh carriage has been provided, a very comfortable one, driven by a juvenile coachman, Ludwig Dennis. He seems quite a boy, but is a sharp and ready little Tyrolese. We can now easily notice that we have left the Tyrol, and are in Italy. The peasants we meet on the road are an ugly, lazy-looking set of beings, and as we go along we notice more and more that the female population are the most hardworked. It is true that the hills on either side of us are covered with vines, and present a very green and fertile aspect, but the fruit orchards are not so fine as in the Tyrol. The road runs all along the Adda valley, and at first is enclosed by lofty mountains, wooded to a great height, but soon the valley contracts and the richer vegetation ceases.

Tirano is reached about one o'clock. We have

lunch here in a miserable little inn. Very little can be said of this place, except that it is dirty, and full of ugly and lazy-looking people. We tried for a long time to find a man who was working or, at any rate, doing something, but it was in vain; they all had their hands in their warm pockets, and were leaning against the wall. Colice is reached in the evening. The road was rather dusty, and the weather hot, so we were glad to forego the pleasure of any views, draw over the hood, and lie back in the carriage. We were delighted to find here a good and comfortable hotel.

July 28. At ten o'clock a.m. we are in the carriage again, *en route* for Como. The weather is gradually getting hot; our drive only takes three hours. We are again compelled to have the hood of the carriage put up; as there is little of interest on the road, little is lost. At about two o'clock we get on the very handsome steamer, "Lombardia," for Como. We are now on this magnificent lake, and it is only from the pen of a great master that an attempt at description can be made of its wonderful beauties. The whole of the lake is bounded by lofty, wooded mountains, rising to a height of seven thousand feet, and the scenery viewed from the deck resembles that of a vast river, both banks being distinguishable. In the forest above, the brilliant green of the chestnut and walnut contrasts with the greyish tints of the olive. Below, numerous gay villas, chiefly belonging to the Milanese aristocracy, surrounded by luxuriant gardens and vineyards, are scattered along the banks of the lake. The lemon and orange trees, the lovely vines, the pretty chapels on the hills, now and again a pretty-looking village, and the lovely azure lake itself, all tell of the beautiful Italian land, extolled by many a poet.

The lake is twelve and a half miles long, two and a half at its greatest width, and one thousand nine hundred feet at its greatest depth. We arrive at Como early in the evening, and go over the town, and stay at Hotel Italia.

July 29. This morning we have to return the same way, by boat, as the previous day, as far as Menaggio, where we disembark, and take the omnibus to Porlazza, a drive of two hours, through a pretty country. This town lies at the extreme end of the beautiful Lake Lugano, which almost rivals that of Como. The boat steams on to Porto, about two and a half hours' run, where we take the diligence to Varese, to the south of the lake, where we stay at the Hotel Varese, a beautiful, first-class establishment, with all possible comforts, and commanding a most extensive view of the Swiss Alps, the Lago Maggiore and Varese. An extensive, very well laid-out park, with grottoes, lawn-tennis grounds, etc., surround the hotel. In fact, it is one of the most charming places imaginable to stay at for rest and comfort. The food is also exceptionally good.

July 30. We start in the morning by carriage to Laveno, about two and a half hours' drive, where we take the boat on the Lago Maggiore to Pallanza. Again the lovely scenery as on Como.

We hire a boat to take us to Isola Bella, about three-quarters of an hour's row. We had not been long on the lake when a big thunderstorm overtook us, and we had to put in for shelter at the Isola Madre, about half way. The storm was soon over, and we rowed on to Isola Bella ; they may well call it " Beautiful Island."

On landing at the pier, we are shown through an enormous chateau, very richly decorated, and handsomely furnished. After visiting the chateau, we are shown over the grounds, the most attractive part of our visit.

The island was once a barren rock, and was converted by Count V. Borromeo into a little paradise. It now consists of lovely gardens, rising on ten terraces, one hundred feet above the lake, containing lemon and orange trees, cedars, magnolias, cypresses, laurels, magnificent oleanders, and many other luxuriant products of a southern clime. We were also shown the enormous cork tree, the camphor tree, the tea plant, and a most extraordinary hanging column of ivy, about four feet diameter, and thirty feet high. The whole place is kept in the best style possible, and belongs still to the very wealthy Borromeo family. The present count, who is quite a young man, was in the garden during our visit. It is also interesting to note that Napoleon I. lived on this island for two seasons. I was glad that we took the trouble of visiting the island, for we were well repaid for our pains. We rowed back to Pallanza, and took the boat to Arona, where we arrived in proper time for the train, 4.10 p.m., for Milan, which was reached at about 6.30. We stop at the Grand Hotel de Milan. We are glad to get rest here, and next morning,

July 31, having received an accumulated mail, in consequence of the quarantines in Egypt, I am all the day busy writing letters. In the evening troubled very much with toothache, and am persuaded to have the tooth drawn; and, not having been able to eat at all, and as I am suffering very much, I resolved to go to the dentist, but unfortunately he was out of town. Called upon another one; not at home. I waited till the next morning.

August 1. I find the dentist in, but have to wait my turn. A great many ladies are waiting here, and by their jovial faces, and the happy and comfortable way in which they are all waiting, it can easily be seen that it is only their false teeth that ache.

The dentist tells me that he must draw two teeth that are in bad condition, which he eventually does, and advises me not to go out to-day. I consequently remain at home, and have thus nothing to relate, except that I am relieved from my agonies.

August 2. Visited La Scala, an opera house, which is closed for performances, but open to visitors in the day. The exterior is not very magnificent. The interior, however, is very grand. The theatre is larger than that at Covent Garden, and will seat over three thousand persons. The man who took us round wished us particularly to notice the construction of this theatre, which throws back sound in a most marvellous manner. We went over the whole house, and were specially interested in the stage, which is immense, and were shown all the arrangements for scene-shifting, etc.

Visited the glorious Cathedral of Milan, a Gothic structure, one of the largest churches in Europe, built entirely of marble, and decorated with ninety-eight turrets, and no less than two thousand marble statues. The interior is very elaborate, with double aisles, borne by fifty-two enormous pillars. The stained-glass windows are very fine, and throw a subdued light on the interior, which is very impressive. The architecture of the edifice is very wonderfully executed, and the labour, which extended over five hundred years, in its construction will be understood in closely examining its elaborate designs. There can be no difference of opinion as to the merits of this magnificent edifice which in every way will rival with any existing cathedral.

One of the modern buildings worthy of note is the Gallerie Vittore Emanuel.

An enormous arcade, the largest of its kind that I have as yet seen, built to a very great height in the shape of a cross, the centre forming a circle, is covered with a fine cupola. The arcade is filled with handsome and inviting shops, cafés, and restaurants.

Every visitor must notice here how fond the Italians are of music. In the summer months, as the opera and theatres are closed, at nearly every café a band is playing the pretty Italian airs; so that the streets of Milan are, so to say, transformed at night to a promenade concert. At the Restaurant Cova, where we dined in the open air, under the shade of palm and orange trees, an excellent band was performing; and here the Milanese gentry congregate in the evenings, to refresh themselves with ices and lemonade. The Italians call Milan the Paris of Italy; and they do so with right, for I was in every way delighted with the place, and will carry away happy recollections from it, of course with the exception of the toothache.

August 3. As an interval of continual sight-seeing, a park is a great relief. The one to which we now drive is very handsomely laid out with a plain but enormous fountain playing in its centre. A fine avenue of trees, and many plants which we are accustomed to see in a stunted form, or under the roof of a conservatory only, here attain an unusual development under the Italian sky. The Museums on either side of these gardens we also visit; they are very good indeed, and contain excellent collections.

We now prepare to leave for Venice, which, after a long ride through the night, we reach at about five o'clock in the morning.

August 4. At the station we take a gondola, of which I shall speak later on, and are safely landed at the Hotel Victoria. Here we are in Venice, the grand old city, that for a thousand years held the foremost position in the history of the world—the city whose very stones have tongues, and whose towers are eloquent. The very briefest catalogue of the events which have rendered this noble city celebrated, would demand a volume. The very schoolboy here could not help calling up a throng of associations of interest regarding its greatness, the splendours of its Courts, and the many terrible tales of the most awful despotism that ever existed. But was Venice famous only for its conquests, its splendour, its cruel secret tribunals, its proud nobles, and so forth! Did not Titian, Tintoretto, Canova, Tasso, Marco Polo, amongst many, many others, live and die here? Was not the first printing press established here, and the first newspaper printed sold in the streets of Venice for a coin called a "Gazzetta"? Gunpowder and artillery were first used by the Venetian soldiers. There is no doubt but that Venice, in her day, was the grandest city. As is well known, we cannot boast here of any streets; horses and cabs, carriages, or any road conveyances are unknown. The gondola is the only thing that runs upon the water-streets. It is very graceful in shape, more like that of a large canoe, with its ends bent up, and forming the shape of half an oval.

The gondolas are all painted black; they were ordered in the fifteenth century to go into mourning in consequence of the plague, and have been kept so ever since. The gondolier uses his oar standing, and pushes it from him, and very rarely lifts it out of the water. He has no rudder, but guides the gondola with his oar, always using it on one side of the boat. The movement looks easy, but is said to be very difficult. The accuracy with which they guide their boats is marvellous. They turn a corner within an inch, do not touch; and they pass in and out on the crowded canals without the least jerk or collision, and can stop suddenly when going at a great speed.

We leave our hotel, and pass through a couple of streets, properly speaking, passages, and suddenly come upon the Piazza San Marco. How many descriptions of this grand place have gone forth from the pens of hundreds of charmed writers! This is the finest place of its kind in Europe.

Before us, on this enormous square, rises the Church of St. Mark, with its five hundred columns of marble, its statues, mosaics, its wondrous arches, its peculiarly shaped domes, the whole looking more like a grand Mahomedan mosque than a Christian church. Close to this rises the huge tower called the Campanile, the pinnacle of which is in the shape of a pyramid, and the summit crowned by a large gilt figure. On our right, in Venetian Gothic style, we see part of the most magnificent Palace of the Doges; on the three sides, an imposing building, with three rows of continuous arcades, formed on each side by one hundred and twenty-nine arches, in which are contained the principal shops of Venice, while the upper parts are a series of palaces. The effect produced upon me here is never to be forgotten.

We now cross the Piazza (six hundred feet by three hundred feet), and ascend the Campanile (three hundred and fifty feet), which is accomplished with little fatigue, as the ascent is made by inclined planes. The view we have from this tower is beyond description. Around us is the labyrinth of canals, the waters of which cannot be distinguished from the masses of high palaces, churches, and other grand buildings which surround them. Just beneath us is the beautiful Church of

St. Mark, and the Square. In the distance on one side, the Alps; on the other, the Adriatic. It was well worth while taking the trouble of ascending.

We now visit the Church of St. Mark. Perhaps in no building has been lavished such costly material as in this. The façade is made up of the architecture of all ages, and is brilliantly adorned with mosaic. The interior is wonderfully impressive, and opens before us as a vast cave hewn in the form of a cross. It seems very dark to us at first, but very soon do we notice its high roof and domes covered with the richest gilt mosaics, and its polished walls, with rich alabaster under foot and overhead, a continual succession of crowded imagery. The whole of this temple is draped with this gorgeous tapestry of stone and these paintings of marble. The most wonderfully executed doors in bronze, and alabaster columns, together with a profusion of statues, pass before us one into the other as in a dream.

This morning we take a gondola, and are gliding along the canals, to and fro, under the small bridges, until we reach the Grand Canal, in which, from one end to the other, the handsomest of palaces, churches, and public buildings rise out of the water. This is the fashionable resort of the Venetians. The most prominent buildings on the way are: the Foscari Palace, one of the finest examples of Venetian architecture; the Palace Ca d'Oro, again a most magnificent structure; the Palaces Pezaro and Vendramin Calergi.

We are so delighted with this canal that we again return to it, and this time are gliding within a few feet of the royal palace, containing the King and Crown Prince of Italy, who had only that day arrived in Venice.

August 5. We to-day visit the grand Palace of the Doges, founded over one thousand years ago, and destroyed again five times, only to be re-built each time on a grander scale. It is in the Venetian Gothic style, the two colonnades, with their pointed vaultings, rich mouldings, and double rows of columns, as well as the handsome pointed fringe along the whole structure, are known too well. We enter by a grand doorway to the court, surrounded by two storeys of arcades, and cross over to the Giant's Staircase, the main entrance to the rooms of the palace. At the top of this staircase, we reach a fine colonnade, having on our right again, a staircase called the Golden Stairs, upon which, in the grand days of Venice, only the nobility, who names were entered in the Golden Book, were allowed to tread. From this most handsomely decorated staircase, we go through a passage into the Hall of the Grand Council. This is a magnificent hall (one hundred and seventy-five feet by eighty-five feet), in which the nobles of Venice sat. The decorations are rich in the extreme: the ceiling covered with fine oil paintings, framed with most elaborate gildings; the four walls are also covered with pictures, one of them, the largest ever painted on canvas, and representing the Glory of Paradise, by Tintoretto, covers the whole wall, that is, a space of eighty-five feet. The rest, covering the side walls, are the great victories of Venice, painted by Tintoretto, Veronese, and Bassano. Above these paintings, all round the hall, are the portraits of the seventy-six Doges, arranged in chronological order. One vacant spot, consisting of a black veil, on which is written in Latin : " This is the place of Marino Faliere, decapitated for his crimes," which he certainly deserved, having laid a plot to murder all the Venetian nobles of Venice, and make himself absolute prince of the State, but was discovered only just in time to be punished.

The Election Hall, in which the ballotings take place, is also a fine hall, full again of marvellous pictures, mostly of Venetian battles.

We now come to the Council Chamber. In this hall, despite its beautiful adornments, a certain awe strikes the visitor, an unaccountable fascination, for here sat the Council of Ten, who gave forth their terrible decrees. Here they sat, with unlimited authority, powerful, relentless, cruel. The outsides of the palace, the entrances of the Grand Hall, the foot of the staircase, had each their lion's mouth, with open jaws, over which was inscribed, " Denounce,

denounce." Into these were placed, without any signature or name of the writer, information, evidence in any shape, denouncing certain persons of crime, treason or otherwise. Once denounced, the limbs of the secret law were set to work, the victim brought, nobody knew when or how, to the Chamber of Ten, and there tried. Visions of strangulation, torture, and the executioner's axe here come before us. The victim, once sentenced, his family miss him, nobody dare ask where he is. In a semicircle pointed out to us, the ten masked men sat, and through secret passages, from the dungeons below, the victim was brought at once face to face with his judges.

Next to this hall is the Room of the Three, who formed a higher Court, more terrible than that of the Ten. Here these masked men sat and listened to the confessions elicited by the rack, and received the answers to questions put to the accused.

We now go through the various reception rooms and private apartments of the Doges, one more elaborate than the other. Returning to the Hall of Three, we pass through a secret doorway into a narrow passage; further on, down a narrow flight of steps leading to the prison cells. On the other side of the canal is a large prison, which is connected with the palace by the Bridge of Sighs, receiving its name from the fact that the prisoner had to pass it on going to trial, and return by it either to prison or death. If released, he would, of course, be liberated without having to cross over to the prison. The prisons are horrible in the extreme. We are glad to quit these black dungeons, and get into the open air again.

We visit the Rialto, mentioned by Shakspere in the "Merchant of Venice," also cross the quaint old bridge of the same name, forming really a row of shops sustained by an arch. Also Palazzo Emo Treves, where we view Canova's magnificent last work, the Statues of Hector and Ajax.

We now go to the Church of St. John and Paul, a very fine building, containing a quantity of tombs and sculptures, the most peculiar one being that of the Doge Andrea Vaudramin.

This being Sunday, the city is in gala, and in the evening we visit the Place St. Mark, with thousands of people promenading, and a band playing in the centre, where we pass a few delightful hours in the cool air, especially after a hot and hard day's work of sight-seeing.

The next morning we arrange to leave for Florence.

August 6. It is a hot day, especially up to three o'clock, during which time we find ourselves compelled, every now and then, to take fresh lemonades. In the afternoon we are, however, more comfortable, and, once past Bologna, the road becomes interesting, for we are rapidly making our way through the Appenines, and passing through about thirty to forty tunnels, every now and then being able to see far into the valley below, until we have made our way down again in the Valley of the Aron, in which, guarded on the north and east by lofty mountains, lies the beautiful city of Florence. We put up at the Hotel de l'Europe.

August 7. We first visit the Baptistry, a heavy octagonal building in black and white marble. The outside of this structure does not demand special description, with the exception of the charming and curious bronze gates. There are three gates. The northern is cast in twenty panels, representing scenes in the life of Christ. The southern, also divided into twenty panels, represents the life of St. John the Baptist; and, lastly, the eastern gate, which is by far the finest, represents scenes of Old Testament history. The framework especially of this gate is simply exquisite, and the delicate designs of foliage, flowers, and other devices form an ornamentation worthy of the great genius Ghiberti.

As seems to be common with Italian churches, so it is found here, that on entering one is displeased with the gloominess; but we soon discover, on looking up into the cupola, that it is covered with extraordinary mosaics of an early date. The designs are rather grotesque, such as the representation of the Devil in the act of devouring a soul.

We now visited the Church of Santa Croce, the

most interesting church in Florence, containing many works of art by the greatest Italian sculptors and painters, and also the resting places and living memories of the greatest men. The building itself is very old, but has been continually restored; in fact, the façade is quite new, and was unveiled in 1863. In front of this cathedral, in white marble, stands the monument of Dante.

The exterior of S. Croce is very impressive and beautiful, nearly the whole being built of white marble. The interior is solemn and grand, and is full of tombs and tablets, statues, and resting-places of great men, especially of Michael Angelo, the great painter, sculptor, and architect, the most variously accomplished man that ever lived; and day after day, as we go on through this great museum of Italy, more and more are we impressed with the grandeur, the marvellous conception, and accomplishments of this man. The monument erected here over his tomb, although of excellent design by Vasari, is not good enough for this gifted man. Second, is the monument to Dante, this great Italian receiving at the hands of his country similar, if not more sincere, treatment than Shakspere. Dante died in 1321, and this monument was erected in 1829. The tomb of Machiavello, the great historian; the monument to Cherubine; and, finally, amongst many others, in this church lies the body of the great Galileo and his pupil Viviani.

A very funny, but excellent guide, took us round this church. "Look at this monument of Dante," says he, "if he arose from the det (dead) he von't tie again." He is right, for it only presents a huge pile of marble, with two ungraceful, immense figures sprawling over it. "Now," says our man, "look dis here, you see what can work de gret Master Canova." And truly, next the monument of Dante, stands this wonderful contrast, erected in memory of Alfiere, a true work of art.

Other exquisite monuments and frescoes are shown here, which, however, I will not attempt to describe.

In the afternoon we took a drive in the Cascine, a very large park. At the extreme end we visited the monument to the Rajah of Kolapore, who died, in 1870, at one of the Florence hotels, when returning from England to India. A monument in Oriental style, supported by four columns, and under the cupola, which surmounts them, stands the bust of this Prince (Rajah Ram Chuttraputti), representing him about one-half larger than life-size, dressed in a magnificent turban of crimson and gold stuff.

August 8. We now visit the Piazza del Duomo, in which stands the Campanile, or bell tower, and the great Florence Cathedral.

How proudly these two gigantic and magnificent structures tower above their surrounding buildings. The whole mass we see before us is constructed of black and white marble, and undoubtedly the order given to the architect, Arnolfo del Cambio, to rear a temple which was to exceed in magnificence anything the world has yet seen, was faithfully carried out.

The dimensions of the Cathedral are five hundred feet in length, and three hundred and eighty-eight in height. The whole is built of splendid marbles, black, white, red, and green, which, under the mid-day sun, give it a very rich appearance, especially with the magnificent designs produced by these various colours. Both the Cathedral and the Campanile are of the same design, and are covered with tablets, reliefs, and statues, the whole conveying to one a majestic beauty which no words can possibly describe.

The Cupola of the Duomo, apart from its enormous size and beauty, was the first double dome built in Europe, and has served as a model ever since. The dome itself sits, as it were, on three other domes. As we enter from the glare into this vast edifice, we find it very dark, our eyes are soon accustomed to the change, and we cannot help looking up with surprise and admiration, firstly at the Cupola. When Michael Angelo was designing St. Peter's in Rome, he was told that he could now surpass the dome of Florence. "I will make her sister dome larger, yes, but not more beautiful," was his reply. If this great artist could not invent or imagine anything more beautiful, is it not sufficient description ? and if not, how is one to describe what the art of man cannot contrive to surpass? The ceiling of the dome is covered with frescoes, and the three other ones with mosaics, having all around long, narrow, painted glass windows, which, when looking around you, turn daylight into a miracle of splendour.

We now visit the Museum, passing through the Piazza della Signoria, which is the most important square in Florence, very fine indeed, and the Colonnade of the Uffizi, forming a double row of columns, and containing a great many statues of the celebrated Italian poets, artists, historians, etc. Above the left colonnade is the Galleria degli Uffizi, or museum. Here I can afford no description, but that it is one of the richest collections in Europe. The various halls run out of one corridor one hundred and seventy-eight yards long! The chief works that I will mention are contained in the Tribune: viz., the celebrated Venus de Medici, the Wrestlers, the Grinder, and the Dancing Fawn.

Dined at Captaini's Restaurant, very good, having also tried the day previous the excellent one of Donney and Neveux.

I must not omit to mention that we also visited the Palazzo Pitti, now the Palace of the King of Italy, in which we were shown through the apartments, containing many treasures of the Medici family. The whole of the Palace is fitted up sumptuously, the grand saloon and the Queen's bedroom being the most splendid.

We start by a midnight train for Rome, which we reach early in the morning.

August. Here we are in the Eternal City, ready to wander through its churches, streets, public buildings and ruins, forming one long chapter of history throughout upwards of two thousand years.

Wherever we tread, our thoughts are continually carried to the contemplation of the past; the ancient centre of western civilization, the city of the republic and empire, on the ruins of which was formed the seat of ecclesiastical jurisdiction and oppression, and now the capital of a progressing European power.

We commence by a visit to St. Peter's Cathedral, standing on the Piazza S. Pietro, enclosed by an imposing colonnade in elliptical shape, and composed of two hundred and eighty-four columns in four rows. Above these columns are one hundred and sixty-two statues of saints. A great obelisk and fountain decorate the centre.

It is as well to have an idea first of the size of St. Peter's, which is the largest church in the world, and, undoubtedly, the most remarkable monument of modern times, no form of art of the greatest men having been forgotten which could contribute to the beauty of this edifice, yea, in which the great men seem to have exhausted their skill. The height of the church is four hundred and thirty-five feet, the length two hundred and five yards, and including porticoes two hundred and thirty-two yards; the diameter of the dome one hundred and thirty-eight feet. Comparing this with St. Paul's in London, viz., length, one hundred and seventy yards, the area of St. Paul's is nine thousand three hundred and fifty square yards, while that of St. Peter's is eighteen thousand square yards. These figures can give one an idea of the enormous size of this building.

Up to the end of the seventeenth century ten million sterling were expended on it. Its maintenance costs seven thousand five hundred pounds per annum. The new additions that have been made, such as the Sacristy, costing one hundred and eighty thousand pounds, would bring the cost as it stands now to most terrific figures. Upon entering this building, the effect produced upon us as a whole is something beyond description. Its vastness cannot at first be realised. The mufic columns, one hundred and forty-eight in number, of solid granite; its four huge buttresses, two hundred and thirty-four feet in circumference, supporting the dome; its marble walls and marble pavements inlaid with designs of great masters; its hundreds of marble statues around, quite bewilder the stranger with delight and astonishment. No paintings adorn this remarkable building, the whole of the dome is one mass of mosaics. At the entrance are four enormous gates of bronze, the panels of which were of Christian work, while the outside fringes and ornaments are ancient, having been the gates taken from the Temple of Venus.

In the centre of the church rises the Canopy, a high altar used for the celebration of Mass on grand days. It is supported by four richly gilded spiral bronze columns, no less than one hundred feet high.

Beneath this, by descending a flight of stairs, we are led to the Shrine. It is of semi-circular shape, and surrounded by eighty-nine large gilt lamps. Here we see the statue, by Canova, of the late Pope, Pius IX., in the attitude of prayer, a most magnificent work of art. Around the statue the walls are inlaid with the choicest marbles and stones, beautifully polished, while in front of it is shown the tomb of St. Peter. It is only on ascending the Cupola that we see now what a gigantic edifice we are in. The colossal statues, sixteen feet high, now appear to us in their true size. Certainly, St. Peter's in Rome must be the edifice among the many I have seen that is the most wonderful and the most beautiful.

Our next visit is to the Pantheon, the best preserved of all monuments of ancient Rome. The portico is supported by sixteen huge granite columns, and in the niches at the sides are colossal statues of Augustus and Agrippa. The roof of the portico, as well as that of the cupola itself, were covered with bronze plates. The height and diameter of the dome are equal, viz., one hundred and forty feet, thus two feet more than St. Peter's. It is of circular shape, and is lighted by a circular open space left in the centre. The whole of this cupola was formerly decorated with bronze work, but was taken down by the Popes, and used to cast the canopy columns for St. Peter's! This act of barbarism, amongst hundreds of others, in destroying the grand history of the ancient Romans, only proved with what fanatical zeal the Popes carried on their government under the cloak of Christianity, usurping the name of religion.

The Pantheon, which should have been a record for ages to come of bygone grandeur, has only its bare walls and roof to show of its immense size and beautiful structure. It is used as a church, and contains the bodies of great artists, etc. The body of Victor Emanuel lies here.

Leaving the Pantheon, we proceed to the Church of S. Maria sopra Minerva, a most magnificent church, the chief attraction, however, being Michael Angelo's splendid statue of Christ bearing the cross.

We go on to S. Maria Maggiori. This is again a most elaborate building, containing a mass of marble and granite almost beyond description. The columns of the façade are enormous; but the central one, sixteen feet in circumference and forty-six feet in height, of one solid piece of granite, being an old column of Constantine, gives one a good idea of what the ancient Romans were capable of doing. The special points of attraction here are the two chapels built by Sixtus V., the amount of mosaics in marble and otherwise, the magnificent gildings of the cupolas. The marvellous decorations here would require pages of description. It is simply wonderful what amount of labour has been bestowed, and what amount of money, shall I say, wasted—well, spent.

Visit Trajan's Forum, a ruin, out of which soars, as if in defiance of time, the wonderful monument of the Column of Trajan, about one hundred and fifty feet high, ornamented with two thousand five hundred human figures and a great quantity of horses, arms, etc., representing the various events of two campaigns of the Emperor.

Visit Forum Romanum. Perhaps no spot in the world contains within the same compass an equal number of interesting ruins. To our right and left, covering an enormous area, we look down upon nothing but one mass of ruins. Remains of enormous columns lie strewed on the ground; huge pieces of pillars have been placed to indicate the positions where once the actual columns stood. Above us are towering rows of magnificent columns that must have once decorated the most beautiful of buildings. A grand triumphal arch of Septimius Severus is still left to record bygone grandeur. The temple of Castor and

Pollux, the temples of Cæsar, Venus, Vesta, Faustina, Saturn, Vespasian, all in ruins, only here and there a column or two or three walls are left. The amount of ruins here are beyond description.

Visit the gigantic ruins of the Colosseum, or amphitheatre, completed by Titus about eighteen hundred years ago, being still, in its ruins, one of the most imposing structures in the world. This theatre was large enough to seat eighty-seven thousand persons. It was of an oval shape, one-third of a mile in length. The height is one hundred and fifty-six feet, and the arena ninety-three yards by fifty-eight yards. It is built of very large blocks of stone, held together by iron cramps, which have, however, long since been removed to be used for the building of churches. The grand, or Emperor's, entrance is still to be seen, also the vaults which contained the wild beasts, the rooms of the gladiators, and the cells of the prisoners. Parts of the tiers of seats are distinguishable. Although only one-third of the gigantic structure remains, the ruins are still stupendously impressive.

Close to the Colosseum stands the Triumphal Arch of Constantine, the best-preserved structure of the kind, and this, no doubt, in consequence of his having declared himself in favour of Christianity. This arch was used by Napoleon I. as model for that of the Arc de Triomphe in Paris.

We now visit the Church of S. Paolo fuori le

Mura (St. Paul's without), which is in reality the finest and most interesting church in Rome. One Pope after another seems to have done something to restore and embellish this beautiful building. An enormous sum of money was left by the late Pope to complete the entrance, which is still unfinished.

As we enter, we notice at each end of the transept a sumptuous altar of malachite, which was a gift of Nicholas I. of Russia, to the Pope. Four magnificent columns of Egyptian alabaster carry the canopy of the high altar. These, together with two other columns of the same kind, placed at the new principal entrance, were presented by the Khedive of Egypt to the same Pope. The nave and the aisles, supported by eighty granite columns, each seventy feet high, are imposing from their vast dimensions and the valuable materials with which they are built. Around this part of the building, above the columns, two hundred and sixty medallions in rich mosaics, representing all the Popes of Rome, each five feet in diameter, attract our attention, especially, also, the richly carved and decorated ceilings.

Returning to the body of the church, we see under the arch the High Altar, with a canopy most luxuriantly decorated with coloured rare marbles, alabasters, and other stones, under which the Apostle Paul is supposed to be buried.

The decorations of this wonderful church—which

is built entirely of marble, its floors, also, being paved in mosaics of marble in divers colours, and polished so that it looks more like glass than anything else; its masses of mosaics, bronzes, precious stones, decorations, all carried out by great masters, in the most expensive manner possible—exhaust all interest one may have, or pleasure that may be derived from similar works of art that can be seen, and which we visited, in various other churches at Rome.

It is impossible to describe all the churches, with their treasures or works of art, so that a list of the principal ones, with a note, will be sufficient.

S. Paolo alle Tre Fontane (the three fountains), built on the traditional spot where St. Paul suffered martyrdom, and where three springs are said to have welled at the places touched by the head of the Apostle when he was executed. Three immense columns mark these spots.

S. Pietro in Vincoli, where, in the sacristy of a chapel with bronze doors, the chains with which St. Peter was chained are kept, and exhibited once a year to the public. In this church is the famous and most magnificent statue of Moses, adorning the monument of Pope Julius II., by Michael Angelo.

S. Maria degli Angeli, containing a colossal statue of St. Bruno and a great number of beautiful paintings. Of special note are sixteen granite columns, of

Oriental granite, each forty-five feet high and sixteen feet in circumference.

S. Maria in Aracoeli, containing beautiful frescoes, and built on twenty-two ancient granite columns.

S. Giovanni Laterano has a magnificent and imposing façade and portico. The ceiling, of most elaborate workmanship, decorated in bronze gilt; most wonderfully ornamented canopy, carried by alabaster columns; extraordinary decorations in marble and precious stones, mosaics, paintings, and also two enormous bronze gilt columns.

Also visited S. Maria della Pace and S. Croce in Gerusalemme.

S. Maria della Concezione, containing the most beautiful and famous picture, by Guido Reni, of the Angel St. Michael. This church belongs to the Capuchin Fathers, who occupy the adjoining convent. Underneath this church are four large burial vaults, in which we were shown, by one of the monks, the bones of about four thousand departed Capuchins, arranged and decorating the vaults in a most ghastly manner. Arches built of skulls, supported by columns built of bones; ceilings decorated with knee-caps, shoulder-blades, small joints, etc. In each vault are a few tombs (of earth brought from Jerusalem); and in the case of a new interment, when all the tombs are full, the bones which have been the longest undisturbed are dug out, scraped and cleaned, to be used for decoration in the manner indicated. The monk who showed us this ghastly sight seemed to plume himself on what, I supposed, must have been their good taste and architectural genius. I was glad to hear that Victor Emanuel put a stop to any further display of their decorative tastes.

S. Pietro in Montorio, a small church, built, it is supposed, on the spot where St. Peter suffered martyrdom. The monk in charge was good enough to give me some of the sand in which the cross upon which the saint was crucified was supposed to have been erected.

Scala Sancta, or Holy Staircase, a flight of twenty-eight steps, of marble, supposed to have been the original ones in Jerusalem in the palace of Pontius Pilate, and on which every person ascending must do so on his knees—two other staircases on each side of the holy one for the descent. From the number of people who have crawled up these steps, they have been worn down in a marvellous manner, but are now protected with a covering of wood.

These are some of the principal churches we visited in Rome, which contains at the present moment no less than three hundred and sixty, nearly all founded on some miserable superstition, mostly built in the most lavish style imaginable, each Pope trying to excel the other in sacred buildings; while, on the other hand, poor-houses, hospitals, or other necessary buildings, are very scarce, and then only modern.

Time after time, as we leave a magnificent edifice, we turn down a lot of filthy streets containing the most miserable specimens of humanity; one hundred churches less, and the money expended in real charity, would undoubtedly have been doing more to the praise of the Almighty.

But not only were these the edifices the Popes were contented with, but in order to adorn the churches, and also, as they maintained, to destroy any remains of Paganism in holy Rome; all the glorious monuments, edifices, temples of incalculable grandeur and value were destroyed; but, curiously enough, their granites, marbles, bronzes, precious stones, even some of their gates, were bodily used for the building and decoration of the churches.

We now turn towards the Vatican Palace. Originally a dwelling-house of the Popes, it is now, so to say, a town by itself, and contains no less than eleven thousand halls, chapels, saloons, and private apartments, and where the dreaded, terrible, and powerful court of the Popes held its sway. Now, however, things have altered, Rome is under the Italian Government. The Papal dominion reaching only within the Vatican walls, according to a law passed by Victor Emanuel in 1871. A small body of Swiss Guards, in their quaint costume, as we enter, are to be seen, for they seem to be acting a burlesque on the departed power and grandeur of their master.

The Sistine Chapel contains a great number of frescoes by old masters, and the decoration of the dome, painted by Michael Angelo, is a marvellous work, and makes one fully aware of the importance of this great man, not only as a painter and sculptor, but also as an architect, for the way in which the various Biblical scenes are connected by an imaginative structure with columns, pillars, bronzes, etc., is beautiful beyond description.

Visited the great and celebrated Museum of the Vatican, enormous in size, which cannot now be described; a few of the most important things must be remembered.

In the Library (the largest in the world, part of which is located in a hall three hundred and eighteen yards long) we saw the famous Vatican Bible. In the Picture Gallery, Raphael's "Madonna," and his last work, the "Transfiguration." In the Gallery of Antiquities, the Group of Laocoon, Apollo Belvedere, the Apoxyominus (an athlete cleaning his arm), Minerva Medica, and the Venus of the Vatican.

In order to form an idea of the immense size of the Museum, and the wonderful and beautiful things collected by the various Popes, the enormous quantity of presents they received from all parts of the globe, and the sumptuous buildings which contain all these treasures, it would take a complete volume to describe them.

Visited the huge ruins of the Baths of Caracalla, the magnificence of which must have been unparalleled. The bare walls are only left. Huge columns, richly adorned, and a great deal of beautiful mosaic pavement, all this left only as witnesses of the grandeur that must have been here sixteen hundred years ago. Certain parts of these baths are certainly still to be distinguished, such as the vapour, the warm, and the cold baths; the latter must have been the most beautiful, built in circular shape. These baths could accommodate sixteen hundred bathers.

We now visit the Capitol, which stands on the most important site of Rome, for about two thousand five hundred years ago a temple was erected here, which, however, was destroyed four hundred years afterwards. It was rebuilt in much grandeur, only to be destroyed again, and robbed of its gilded bronze tiles in 455 by the Vandals.

The present form of the Capitol dates, however, from the sixteenth century, after having formed the centre of civic administration for over four hundred years.

The entrance to the Capitol is very fine, the general plan having been restored and carried out by Michael Angelo. At the top of a very wide staircase, at the bottom of which two enormous Egyptian lions are cut out of basalt, are the colossal figures of Castor and Pollux, standing beside their horses. This staircase leads into the Capitol, and faces the beautiful square, in which rises the admirable statue in bronze of Marcus Aurelius. The interior is mostly of modern restoration, and contains a very good Museum, in which I saw the wonderful Greek Statue of the Dying Gladiator, and the Capitoline Venus, also of Greek workmanship.

These are the buildings and ruins of Rome which afford most interest, although there are still many other sights well worth our trouble of having seen, but which, if they had to be all described, would require too much space and time. The city itself, since the occupation by Victor Emanuel, is steadily improving, and especially in the new quarter, the handsome Via Nationale being a very magnificent street. But the old town is, beyond description, filthy, the streets narrow, and the houses miserable.

Coming out of a grand church immediately into a most wretched street, is a contrast not to be forgotten, and it is to be hoped that the present Government will continue to repair all the evils produced by mismanagement of its predecessors.

August. We leave this morning for Naples. "See Naples and die," is the Italian saying; and as we are nearing the town, the Mount Vesuvius, on our left, is already visible, throwing out his smoke and vapours, and blackening the blue sky above.

The hotel we stop at is the " Metropole," facing the sea, and the view from the bedroom window, as well as the fresh breeze blowing in, is very delightful.

While we were at Como, we had heard, and afterwards read, of a great calamity that had taken place on the island of Ischia, near Naples. The details were terrible, for it was said that five thousand persons had lost their lives through an earthquake having buried them under the debris of their demolished houses. We made up our minds to visit the scene of the disaster, and upon hearing that a boat was leaving the next morning, we engaged a guide to take us there. A permit from the Prefect of Police had to be obtained before leaving, which our guide duly procured.

August. The steamer was densely packed, mostly by people who were bent on business. Some had lost their property; others had lost friends, and perhaps dear relations; here and there could be seen a woman, a man, a child in deep mourning, no doubt the woman for her husband, the man for his wife, and perhaps the child for its parents.

As we steam away from Naples pier and look back on the town, the view that strikes the eye is lovely beyond description. The beautiful semi-circular bay has perhaps no rival in the world. The town is built on the whole extent of the bay, and with the green-covered hills in the distance, a deep blue sky above, and the sun throwing its powerful rays upon the whole, forms a magnificent panorama.

In about a couple of hours the island of Ischia becomes visible behind one or two other islands, which we have now passed. We steer round the island for the town, or I should say the ruins, of Casamicciola. At first sight, in the distance, nothing is noticed of the ruins.

The houses on the hill seem to be all standing in the beautiful gardens and groves which surround them. The whole island is very beautiful and fertile, and Casamicciola in particular; and it is not to be wondered at that this spot was chosen as the chief resort for travellers, and gradually developed into a fashionable watering place.

As we come off the steamer, we first see an enormous quantity of wooden sheds, which have been put up for the relief of the homeless. We are, however, anxious to see the ruins, and do not linger here.

It is only on being on the spot that the enormity of the disaster can be realized. We stand on a huge pile or mound of rubbish crushed into powder, through which may be visible part of the furniture, or perhaps one blank wall only is left to tell the truth that this was once an inhabited house.

We now go along the street of this unfortunate place, and I really do not know how to describe the wreck around me. No modern artillery could accomplish such perfect devastation. Here is a charity school, built with enormous walls of large blocks of stone; its strength seems to have been of little use, for here it is a complete ruin—a grave of many children and some Sisters of Mercy.

Further on we view the ruins of the Hotel Manzi. This seems to have been the most fortunate of buildings, for, at the time that the earthquake took place, there were eighty-three travellers in the hotel, and not one of them was lost. In fact, it was only the kitchen which completely gave way, and buried some of the servants of the hotel, while the other part is cracked and partly broken, and, from day to day, is tumbling in more and more. The son of the proprietor was kind enough to show us over the wreck of his property, and we went through the lower rooms, which still looked safe. He told us that he was on the island during the catastrophe, and said it was about half-past nine p.m., when he was in the office, and a lady residing in the hotel asked him to go with her to the post-office. They had not left the hotel ten minutes, when suddenly they felt a terrible shock, accompanied by a noise resembling several claps of thunder or a prolonged cannonade. They were in the middle of the street, fortunately enough, for the houses had fallen in all directions. The dust arising from the falling in of the houses almost blinded them, and, together with the suddenness of the disaster, as well as the terror they were in at the time, they could hardly realize what had occurred, and simply ran along the streets, they knew not whither. The whole thing, he says, could not have lasted more than ten seconds; but it must have been impossible for any survivor to tell exactly what really happened. He told us that although his property is absolutely lost, still their family is well off; but that the owner of the other hotel is perfectly ruined, having, the year previous, refurnished and decorated his hotel; in fact, he had put all the money he had in the world into this property, called the Picola Santinella. This sad state of affairs is pretty well the same thing all over the island, for the inhabitants have lost all; but what is more terrible is the loss of life—mothers who have lost their husbands, and children who are left with no relations whatever, and in many cases families completely lost.

Not only is the whole town one heap of ruin and destruction, but the roads, even, are broken open with enormous cracks ten and fifteen feet deep; even trees were actually rooted out by the shock. The soldiers were brought to the scene as soon as possible, in order to try and save some of the poor unfortunates buried in the ruins. A good many were saved, and some found sheltered under the ruins in most miraculous positions. In the Picola Santinella Hotel, which is now one heap of ruins, eight English travellers, as well as some members of the best families of Naples, lost their lives. We met the uncle of Count d'Alvi, who had gone in search of the Count's body, which they found, after seven days, in the ruins. This terrible scene of disaster, together with the fearful stench of decomposing bodies lying in the ruins, made a deep impression on us. It is altogether a sad sight, never to be forgotten. We return again to Naples in the afternoon, and in the evening go to the concert at the Public Gardens.

August. To-day we get up at four a.m., to go to Pompeii. We take the train, which runs up within close reach of the ruins. This is, again, the scene of a terrible disaster, but not so terrible a one as that on the Island of Ischia.

Nearly two thousand years ago, the inhabitants of Pompeii were suddenly visited with a fearful shower of hot pumice stones, succeeded by another of ashes, and then an outpour of boiling water from the crater of Mount Vesuvius, above them. The disaster did not come suddenly upon them, so that most of the inhabitants, numbering about thirty thousand, had time to escape, and even to save a good deal of their treasures and other valuables. The mass formed over the town—viz., pumice-stone, water, and ashes—enclosed the ruins as if they were in an air-tight composition, so that the remains of the streets and buildings are preserved to this day in as perfect a state as they were nearly two thousand years ago. It is wonderfully interesting to be strolling through the ancient city, as if it were only yesterday that the inhabitants had quitted the town. The streets, with their names, pavements, and even marks of carriage wheels, are as fresh as ever they were at that time. While the private houses are very interesting, one in particular, that of the tragic poet, with its beautiful mosaics and frescoes, is wonderfully preserved; the reception, sitting, and bed-rooms are quite distinguishable, and are all beautifully decorated, only somewhat small.

The baths are also very interesting, very well divided and proportioned, consisting of cold, hot, and vapour baths. A point worth notice here is, that they used lead pipes and brass taps, with keys of exactly the same kind as used at the present day. The Temples of Venus, Mercury, Jupiter, and Augustus, are still beautiful and interesting. The Amphitheatre, large enough to contain twenty thousand spectators, as well as the Comic Theatre, are well preserved. On the whole, this ancient town was one of the most interesting places I have visited on the Continent.

The Museum of Naples contains most of the statues, bronzes, and relics found at Pompeii. We therefore paid that a visit in the course of the day, and it was wonderfully curious to notice how far advanced in civilization the Romans must have been so many years back.

We drove through this beautifully-situated city, and, like everybody else who has been here, were charmed with the beautiful situation of "Naples the beautiful." The Neapolitans are a specially bright and gay people, and this being Sunday, or at least a fête day, the whole of the town was in the evening in the public promenade, where a concert was being given by a military band. The splendid cafés around were swarming with gaily-dressed people enjoying, with us, the excellent Neapolitan ices. The city itself is not very fine or well-built, whereas the new part of the town, which extends a considerable distance along the quay, is very handsome, and contains, besides the grand gardens and beautiful carriage drives, very many handsome edifices. All the first-class hotels are also in this part of the town, as was also the one which we stayed at (Metropole). Our stay here was all the more agreeable, as our rooms were facing the sea.

August. We have now to return by our old route to Rome, as there is no other way of getting north. The railway arrangements in this country seem to be in a very backward state. Trains are very few, and run at unearthly hours; and in consequence we find ourselves compelled to stay one night at Rome, and go on to Pisa by the following morning's train. The journey, however, from Naples being somewhat fatiguing, the bad arrangements of the Italians, as we choose to style them, come in rather handy, and were a good excuse for not continuing the journey the same night, but taking another rest at the Hotel Continental in Rome.

We are now off by the morning train for Pisa. It is a more pleasant journey than we had yesterday. The day is cold, and every now and then we get a glimpse of the Mediterranean, the railway at times running close to the shore, refreshing us with a delightful breeze. On arriving at Pisa in the evening, put up at the Grand Hotel Minerva.

This quiet town, were it not that it contains one of the seven wonders of the world, would be, for the ordinary traveller, of little importance. Like most Italian towns, it certainly has great historical interest, being one of the oldest, and having especially occupied an important position in the history of art; but all its ancient monuments, with the exception of perhaps a few scanty relics, have disappeared, and it is left to be visited only for the sake of viewing its Cathedral, and, above all, the famous Leaning Tower. This, of course, is the first thing that we start to visit.

This extraordinary tower is of a circular form, and rises in eight different stories to a height of about one hundred and eighty feet. It is built thirteen feet out of perpendicular, and the first impression one has of it is, that it seems in a very unsafe state, liable at any minute to fall over. The question whether this peculiar oblique position was intentional or accidental seems to be unsettled. It is, however, supposed that the foundations settled during the course of construction, and that in order to remedy the defect as much as possible, an attempt was made to give a vertical position to the other part. The Italians, of course, do not admit this, but put it down as done intentionally, and as a proof of the great skill of the architect, Tommase Pisano.

The Cathedral, which stands on the same grounds as the tower, is a very fine structure, being constructed entirely of white marble, with black and coloured ornamentations. The interior is covered by sixty-eight old Roman and Greek columns, captured by the ancient Pisians in their wars. In the centre of the nave hangs a bronze lamp, only interesting from the fact that it suggested to Galileo, while singing in the choir, through its swaying backwards and forwards, the idea of the pendulum.

The Baptistry, which stands close to the Cathedral, is also worth a visit. It is built entirely of marble, but its exterior has a somewhat heavy and clumsy appearance. The interior, however, is very fine; its huge dome, supported on half pillars, is very imposing. A very fine echo is to be heard here. The half-a-dozen cracked notes produced by our guide resounded in a beautiful distinct chord.

We now visit the Campo Santo, or burial ground.

After the loss of the Holy Land, one of the Archbishops conveyed here fifty-three ship-loads of earth from Jerusalem, so that "the dead might repose in holy ground"! This earth is surrounded by an arcade in Gothic style, one hundred and thirty-eight yards long and fifty-seven yards wide; it contains a large number of monuments and tombs, some of very fine workmanship, but really of little interest.

In the afternoon we take train for Genoa, running along the Riviera de Levanta. This peculiar line runs through striking scenery, along the rugged coast, by means of cuttings and tunnels, of which we traverse no fewer than eighty, some of them of considerable length, and that in the short space of four and a half hours. We arrive at Genoa late in the evening, and stay at the Hotel de la Ville.

Genoa is called by the Italians "la Superba" (the Superb). The beauty of its situation, rising as it does above the sea in a wide semicircle, justly entitles it to this name or distinction; but it is only from this point of view that its superbness can be realized. It certainly contains a few most magnificent streets and structures, but it must be admitted that the inner part of the city, consisting of very narrow streets and miserable houses, together with very badly-constructed drainage, tends to destroy the fascination of the beauty of its situation and the interesting reminiscences of its ancient magnificence.

Genoa is a very busy town; commercially speaking, the most important in Italy. The harbour, which I visited this morning, is on a semicircular bay about two miles in diameter, and was full of all kinds of craft. St. Lorenzo, the cathedral of Genoa, is a very handsome structure, built partly of black and white marble, with massive towers; but after the magnificent edifices I have seen in Italy, I do not think this one deserves very special notice. A drive through the town brings us through two magnificent streets, Via Garibaldi and Via Roma, the former being flanked by a succession of palaces, the most important being that of Palazzo Rosso, formerly the property of an Italian nobleman, but now transformed into a picture gallery and library.

The favourite drive here is the Aqua Sola, a very handsome park, with fountains, lakes, etc., the whole laid out in very fine style.

The statue of Christopher Columbus, who is said to have been born close to Genoa, stands on one of the large squares, and represents the great discoverer leaning on an anchor. The pedestal is adorned with ships' prows, under which kneels the figure of America. The whole is executed in white marble, and is very fine indeed.

The Campo Santo of Genoa (Burial Ground) is about one and a half miles out of the town. I drive there in a carriage, and I must say it was well worth the trouble of visiting. The whole arrangement of this remarkable enclosure is very tasteful and beautiful. It is more like an exhibition of handsome works of art than a burial ground. Each tomb or family vault has a monument erected in memory of the dead which lie beneath it, each in their various galleries, which are built one above the other, and kept apart for men, women, and children's bodies. In the centre there is a very large statue of the Virgin blessing the dead.

This morning we take the train for Nice, *en route* for Monaco. This is one of the most delightful rides imaginable, for the train runs all the way along the sea shore ; while, on the other side, the fruitful olive groves and wooded country form a beautiful panorama. We reach Ventimiglia at about midday. This is the Italian frontier, so that now we are about entering France again, and must bid adieu to Italy.

The scenery becomes more and more attractive, and we soon pass Mentone. The vegetation is luxuriant, especially between this and Nice, and the lovely villas dispersed upon the hills, surrounded by orange and lemon groves, interspersed with palms, fig-trees, and olives, with here and there a beautiful palm growing under the strong sun of southern France as if in the centre of Africa, convert the whole line into one extensive garden. We reach Nice in the afternoon, and soon are driving down the well-known Promenade des Anglais.

Nice has no museums, grand buildings, or monuments, to boast of. Its importance has only been created through the collecting of invalids especially, and other persons, from all parts of Europe, the excellence of its climate in the winter months, its beautiful situation on the Mediterranean, together with the extreme fertility of the soil, which contains all kinds of tropical plants growing to perfection, rendering a stay in this beautiful place most agreeable and invigorating. The place was certainly somewhat deserted during the time I saw it, but I can well understand that any person having once passed the winter here will always long again for it.

The Promenade des Anglais is one of the finest carriage drives in Europe. It is bordered with extensive hotels and villas on the one side, while the other, which stretches along the sea coast, is planted with palms.

We now visit Monaco, where we go to the Hotel des Bains, in the town itself; and in the afternoon visit the famous Monte Carlo.

Monaco is situated on a bold, prominent rock, close to the sea-shore, and is the capital of the diminutive principality, still belonging to the Prince of Monaco, who exercises sovereign rights over his few acres. His capital contains no less than fifteen hundred inhabitants. His palace is an enormous building, which could hold, no doubt, all his (loyal?) subjects.

A pleasant walk up the steep hill above us, leads to the beautiful gardens and grounds, as well as to the Casino itself. To describe the beauty of the gardens here would be almost impossible, no trouble and expense have been spared to make the garden most elaborate and complete. The climate here, of course, helps to the production of all tropical plants, which are arranged in the most tasteful style possible.

We now enter the Casino, or I should say, try to enter, for it seems to be a very hard matter to get in. We are stopped at the door, and requested to procure a ticket. For that purpose we are ushered into an office, where we are first asked for our passports; not having taken these with us, we reply we have none. The young gentleman (?) or what shall I call him, for he belongs to the gang who are running the gambling tables, well, let us say, the gentlemanly-looking young man in charge, shrugs his shoulders, but says he will call the manager. He does so, and we are now faced by a gentlemanly-looking old man. It takes a long time to convince him that we are really strangers, and that our names, etc., are really those which we state them to be. He finally honours us with tickets, which are available for the day only, and are styled as personal tickets of the Strangers' Club.

We now enter into a most magnificent saloon, of very large dimensions, preceded by a handsome antechamber, serving as cloak-room, etc. The grand saloon, most elaborately fitted up, and handsomely decorated, contains eight large tables, placed at distances of twenty-five or thirty feet apart, at which the various gambling games are taking place.

We stand at one of the roulette tables to watch the game proceeding. Here they are, busily placing the stakes, according to their means, on the various numbers or colours. "The game is ready," cries the man in the centre, who is styled the "banker," and round goes a roulette disc to decide the fortune of the excited players.

We can easily distinguish the old hands from the younger and less experienced players. Here is an elderly man who has evidently made it a business to play. There is not the slightest amount of excitement visible in him, he seems to play as if he were paid to do it; perhaps he is, goodness knows. Next to him sits a handsome, well-dressed young lady, her eyes glistening with a feverish excitement as she is placing her stakes and taking in her winnings. She is in luck's way, and has won a good deal, and every turn of the roulette seems to bring her in more. The banker smiles as she draws in her gold, no doubt he thinks, "we shall have all this back to-morrow." At the end of the table sits another creature, she is about sixty, let us flatter her, and call her fifty; she must be an old hand at this game, for she seems very steady in her play. Her hands, covered with jewels, do not betray the slightest amount of nervousness, her freshly-painted face only shows that she is a little put out as she asks the banker to change her another note of one thousand francs. This is the third she has changed, and when there is no more "change left," she tries to smile, and muttering, "no luck," rises, perhaps to try her luck at another table. The only question one must ask oneself is, who is she? or what can she be? But she is not the only one here. Dozens, nay scores, of the same kind are about.

The next table is one played with heavy stakes. A young Russian has just come to play with a handful of bank notes. What miserable luck this young man has, and still he goes on, in less than half an hour he has lost over eight hundred pounds, and he still goes on; well, he hesitates a little now. He puts down eighty pounds, they are swept away. He rises now, thinking, no doubt, he has had enough. Look at this young man standing at the table, watching the game with a kind of vacant stare and a heavy frown on his face, his hands in his pockets; no doubt they were full of money a short time ago, and now they are all emptiness.

The number of young people, especially women, and a great many of most respectable-looking people playing here is most astonishing. What a sad spectacle the whole of this miserable hell, this school of crime, presents, and more especially does one feel this upon going out of the Casino into the beautiful gardens around it, a real hell in the centre of a little paradise.

We were astonished to find so great a number of visitors here, as it is not the season. The hundreds of chairs in the garden around the kiosque of a good band were every one of them occupied. Most splendid hotels, cafés, and restaurants surround the Casino, and the view from the terrace facing the sea is superb.

We stay overnight at the Hotel des Bains in Monaco, and leave the next morning for Marseilles. Here we stop at the Hotel du Louvre et de la Paix, one of the best hotels in the place.

Marseilles is the principal seaport of France, and the depôt of a brisk maritime traffic with India, England, and Africa. The chief attraction of the city is its extensive harbour and docks, principally the Port de la Joliette, the starting point of all the steamers; Basin des Docks, Basin Nationale, and Basin de Radoub. The old harbour is long and narrow, and the entrance is defended by Forts St. Jean and Nicholas, near which is the consigné, or the office of the quarantine authorities.

Close to the harbour is the Cathedral, a new structure, built of black and white stone. The towers are surmounted by domes, and a splendid view is to be had of the Basin de la Joliette from the terrace of this cathedral.

The principal street of Marseilles is La Cannibière,

which intersects the town from west to east. The Bourse, or Exchange, a handsome building with a portico of Corinthian columns, stands in this street.

At the end of the Boulevard de Longchamp is the new handsome building called Musée de Longchamp, consisting of two extensive buildings, adorned by a fountain in the centre. The right wing contains the Museum of Natural History, and on the left is the Picture Gallery. The well-kept grounds at the back of the Museum extend to the Zoological Gardens.

From this we started for the Church of Notre Dame de la Garde, situated on an eminence to the south of the old harbour. The interior contains an image of the Virgin and innumerable votive tablets, presented by those who have been rescued from shipwreck or disease.

The terrace in front of the church, and especially the gallery of the tower—ascended by a flight of one hundred and fifty-four steps, which contains a huge bell weighing ten tons, and is crowned with a large figure of the Virgin—command an admirable view of the city, the harbour, and the barren group of islands at its entrance. I returned to my hotel, driving through the Promenade de Padro, Chateau des Fleurs, descending to the sea, and passing over the Chemin de la Corniche.

Starting next day for Lyons, by the Paris, Lyons.

and Mediterranean Railway, we arrive there after a run of about eight hours, and put up at the Hotel de Toulouse. This fine city is situated on the junction of the rivers Rhone and Saone, and is considered one of the best built towns in France. The Saone is crossed by nine, and the Rhone by eight bridges, and the city is defended by eighteen forts.

The beauty of this city is seen from the height of Fourviere Hill, crowned by its handsome church. This hill is ascended by a Wire Rope Railway, which starts near St. Jean Cathedral. Another place of interest is the Place des Terreaux, in which the Hotel de Ville (Town Hall) and the Museum are situated. The Town Hall is a handsome edifice recently restored.

There are many interesting pictures and statues in the Museum, but more interesting and instructive were the illustrations of silk culture. Next we saw the Civic Library, which contains one hundred and eighty thousand volumes, and one thousand three hundred MSS.

Leaving the Library, we go through two magnificent new streets, viz., Rue de la Republique and Rue de l'Hotel de Ville, and reach Place Bellecour, one of the most spacious squares in Europe, and adorned with an equestrian statue of Louis XIV.

In the Boulevard du Nord, on the left bank of the Rhone, lies the handsome Musée Guimet. It consists chiefly of idols and other objects connected with the religious rites of ancient and modern times. Near the Musée Guimet is the Park de la Fête d'Or, one of the most charming parks I ever visited. It contains rare plants, hot-houses, pleasure grounds, artificial lakes, lawns most tastefully arranged, shady drives and walks, which reminded me of the Bois de Boulogne at Paris.

We return to our hotel in the evening, and dined at the Hotel Universe, and saw the country fair till midnight, and left early next morning for Paris, where we arrive after a run of six hours. We stayed in Paris for three days, and visit the Trocadero, Bois de Boulogne, and left for London *via* Calais, arriving at the Charing Cross Station the same evening, and thus completed a long tour of three months on the Continent of Europe.

SCOTCH TOUR.

AFTER spending three months on the Continent of Europe, I arrived safely in London on the night of the 26th of August, 1883. From this time up to the 5th of September, I spent my time in seeing the Zoological Gardens, Madame Tussaud's Wax Works, the Royal Kew Gardens; visited the premises of Silber and Fleming, David Corsar's, Brotherton and Co.'s, and of various other merchants and manufacturers. I dined at Simpson's and old Albion Taverns, at Holborn and St. James's Restaurants. Saw the performance of "Iolanthe," and concerts at the Covent Garden Theatre; had also the pleasure of seeing some amusing features at the London Pavilion.

On the *6th of September*, 1883, I left London for my Scotch tour; I travelled by express train, and arrived at Manchester in the evening. The scenery between Ambergate and Marple, and Matlock to the Big Forest Tunnel, was exceedingly charming.

The express train was going at the speed of sixty miles an hour, and at some parts of the journey it was making seventy-two or seventy-three miles an hour, or twelve and a half miles in nine minutes. Luncheon was served in the Pullman Car, which was fitted up with all modern comforts.

We reached Manchester at five p.m. In the evening we went to see the performance at Folley's Theatre, which was very amusing. Here we met Mr. George, who has composed the song, "Champagne Charlie," and saw the Review of Scotch Brigade by Bonnie Prince Charlie, a young lad of ten years old, which was very nice, and was well got up indeed.

On the next morning, the 7th, we visited the Post Office, Town Hall, the Exchange (a magnificent building), the Assize Court, the Market, and drove over the town. We also visited some of the best shops, such as Lewis's, in Mosley Street and Mosley Square, which is beautifully situated in the heart of the city, where people resort of an evening. After staying two days at Manchester, we started for Edinburgh by the Caledonian Railway. The scenery between Manchester and Edinburgh is not so charming as that between London and Manchester. However, some portion of it was really picturesque, for the hills and valleys were covered with snow and green moss.

We arrived late in the evening at Edinburgh. The next morning we visited the extensive premises of Alexander Haye, the jeweller; and from there we drove up to Edinburgh Castle, where we were taken round and shown every place of interest by the guide. Here I was pleased to see the Ninety-second Gordon Highlanders, commanded by Colonel White, who was once in Kurachi. The birdseye view of Edinburgh you get from the top of this Castle is very pretty and imposing. At the foot of the Castle lay the Princes Park and Waverley Gardens, most tastefully laid out. A little further on, the Firth of Forth is to be seen, with small steamers floating thereon on the other side. The magnificent row of hotels and other buildings situated in Princes Street appear in splendid style. After spending a few hours in seeing the Castle, we drive through the Old Town of Edinburgh; we go through West Bow and High Street (old houses), St. Giles's Church, and Parliament House. Here we saw the pictures of Lord Brougham, Inglis, Cockburn, and of other illustrious personages, and the Royal Exchange.

Parliament House is a very ancient building. It ceased to be used for the assemblage of Parliament after the National Union in 1707; became then the seat of the Court of Session. It retains its great Hall, one hundred and twenty-two feet by forty-nine feet, though it has undergone great changes. The Hall is sixty feet high, with pendant oaken roof and sculptured corbels like those of Westminster Hall, and contains statues of Lords Boyle, Jeffrey, Melville, Forbes, Blair, and Dundas. In Parliament Square, which was long part of a large ancient cemetery, we were shown the grave of John Knox, the great preacher. The spot is now simply marked with a small surface-stone, bearing the initials of his name, and a little further on, in the Canongate, we saw the house where Knox lived, which now belongs to the Town Council.

From this we go to see the Holyrood Palace. This is a fine building, guarded by the Highlanders. It contains Royal private apartments, a picture gallery, and Queen Mary's private apartments, which continue in the same condition as when inhabited by her. Queen Mary's Bedchamber contains her bed and portrait, and here are to be seen portraits of ancient Scottish Kings and Queens. After going through this Palace, and inspecting the renowned old Abbey, which contains the ashes of many crowned personages, we drive up to Arthur's Seat, which is situated on a high eminence, where the Queen and royal family have been on a visit five times. It was mentioned that the Queen went on foot to the summit. We did the same, and got a comprehensive and panoramic view of Edinburgh We next drove through the Queen's Drive, a splendid hilly tract, where we meet with most lovely scenery.

On one side lies Portobello, the watering-place of Edinburgh, and Prestonpans; and on the other, Duddingston Loch. Arthur's 'Seat is about eight hundred and twenty-two feet above the sea-level.

From here we descend, and go through the Prince Consort's Gates, and drive through the handsome Melville Park, and return to our Hotel Windsor, through Princes Street, which is one of the best streets in Edinburgh. It extends for a mile in straight line. The first object which attracts the attention in the street is the elegant Gothic Spire, erected as a monument to the memory of Sir Walter Scott, costing fifteen thousand pounds; and next to it is the statue of Livingstone. We were greatly pleased, in the evening, to hear the sweet strains of music discoursed by the full band of the Gordon Highlanders. The pipers were playing in the concert-room of the Waverley Gardens. We also visited Moss's Theatre, where some selected pieces were sung, to our great amusement.

On the next morning, the *9th of September*, we take a walk through the Prince's Garden, which is situated in the valley, and most beautifully laid out; and it really was a great treat to us. After this, we take the cab down to Leith, which is the commercial and important port of Edinburgh. We walked over the two long Piers, alongside of which lay many steamers. The streets of Leith are spacious and well built, and especially the commercial street is worthy of notice, as also the fine buildings, such as the Parish Church, the Exchange Buildings, Assembly Rooms, and the Court House.

After driving through the town, we go to Portobello, the famous watering-place of Edinburgh. Here we find a beautiful Promenade Pier, projecting across the centre of the beach into the sea, where you can command a beautiful view of the sea. Portobello is a favourite summer residence and bathing-place, and consists of a number of streets and detached villas.

We again return to Edinburgh, *viâ* Queen's Drive, noticing, on our right, the Nelson Memorial, and on the left, the Gaol. In the evening we walked through George Street, another great street of Edinburgh, where we saw the great statues of George IV., of William Pitt, and of the Rev. Dr. Chalmers. We also went to Charlotte Square, where we saw the Monument of the Prince Consort, which is situated in the centre of a garden. It was unveiled by Her Majesty, in the year 1861, and cost about sixteen thousand five hundred pounds.

On the 10th, we start, by the Caledonian Railway, for Stirling, *viâ* Linlithgow, which we reached after an hour's run. We put up at the Royal Hotel, a decent, old-fashioned house. The first thing we saw was the East and West Church, built in fine Gothic style, which was the coronation place of James VI., in his infancy, and is noted for the ministry of the martyr Guthrie and Ebenezer Erskine. We also saw the beautiful modern Cemetery and Gardens, close by; and one gets really fine and the best view of the fields from this place. The next we saw was the famous Stirling Castle, which stands on the precipitous crown of the hill. The view from the battlements is beautiful and extensive, and you can clearly see the Cambuskenneth Abbey, the Wallace Monument, and the Bridge of Allan Valley. I was much pleased to see here the recruits for the Ninety-first and Ninety-third Highlanders.

After driving through the town, and passing by the County Buildings (Courts of Justice), we visit the old Cambuskenneth Abbey, which is now a ruin, represented by a ruined tower. Near it is the burial place of James III. and his Queen. From this we drive to the foot of the William Wallace Monument, which stands on a bold hill.

After examining this monument, we start for Dunblane, *via* Carse of Stirling. There are two mineral wells at Cromlex, and it is becoming a famous summer residence, and is known in connection with Tannahill's song of "Jessie, the Flower of Dunblane." We pass through the most picturesque scenery that can be witnessed. Shortly we reach the Bridge of Allan, a delightful watering-place, with a good view of Stirling. The surrounding country is very charming, and, after driving through the Glen Dunblane, we came to the Cathedral, which is situated on the banks of the River Allan, and built in fine Gothic architecture. After going through this Cathedral, we left for our hotel, arriving there late in the evening.

On the next day, the 11th, we took train for Callander, arriving there after an hour's run. We go to the Dreadnought Hotel, and after partaking of luncheon, and visiting this little town, we start for Loch Katrine, through the Trossachs, in a stage coach and four.

The road from Callander to Loch Katrine commands, nearly all the way, some of the picturesque scenery of Scotland. Here we pass the Loch Annachir, about five miles long, and Loch Achroy, about a mile and a half, and arrive at the Trossachs Hotel, situated at the head of Loch Achroy, surrounded by beautiful mountains covered with green.

Loch Katrine commences from west of the Trossachs, and extends about eight miles in length, and is about three-quarters of a mile broad. Near its foot lies the wooded and romantic Isle of Ellen, the central scene of the "Lady of the Lake," of which I have heard and read so much in my school days, and it is from this isle that the Glasgow Waterworks takes its source, and which were opened by Her Majesty the Queen in 1859. We take a trip up Loch

Katrine in the fine little steamer, "Rob Roy,' and land at Stronachlachar, where another stage-coach and four is ready to convey us to

Inversnaid, and we arrived here after two hours' drive. This is a most charming little spot, situated at the foot of Loch Lomond, and near which are the Falls of Inversnaid river, which is a magnificent sight, worth seeing. It makes a fine cascade of thirty feet in the immediate neighbourhood of Loch Lomond. Inversnaid on Loch Lomond is the scene of Wordsworth's poem of the "Highland Girl." We put up at the Inversnaid Hotel, and at once take a small boat and make an excursion on Loch Lomond, and visit the famous cave of Rob Roy. After this we return to our hotel, and start next day (12th) for Balloch Pier by the Loch Lomond steamer, the "Prince Consort." The scenery on the Loch Lomond was charming in the extreme.

After steaming for six hours, we arrived at Balloch Pier *viâ* Tarbert, where a train was ready to take us to Glasgow, which city we reached after a run of two hours. We put up at St. Enoch's Hotel, a most magnificent edifice, built at the railway station. Here I met my old friend, Mr. J. Campbell, who was very kind enough to show me round Glasgow in the course of the day. We visited the Cathedral, the Industrial Exhibition, the Public Park, and drove round the city. In the evening, saw the performance of "Silver Gilt" at the Royalty Theatre.

The next day we left for Oban, by the magnificent steamer "Columba." We go by the river Clyde, and here we had the opportunity of witnessing the extensive shipbuilding yards, and the number of vessels that were loading and unloading cargo for different parts of the world. I never witnessed such a forest of ships and steamers anywhere before. We leave the "Columba" at noon, and take a small canal steamer, "Linnett," and pass through the Crinan Canal. At four p.m. we take another large steamer, the "Iona," and go through the Jura Sound, and reach Oban in the evening.

Our steamer made a grand *entrée* into the Bay of Oban, as Highland sports and a regatta were going on there in the presence of Mr. and Mrs. Gladstone and other noblemen. We stayed for two days in Oban, and left for Ballachulish by steamer "Mountaineer," and we reach there by two p.m.

We take a coach and go to Glencoe. Here you see one of the gloomiest, wildest, and most impressive of the sceneries of a Highland glen. The aspect is one of the wildest grandeur that you can possibly behold. The natural mountain ramparts are craggy, abrupt, and tortuous, and the glen abounds in caverns, fissures, and cliffs, that shut out the light of day. After admiring this grand scenery of nature, we return to our steamer, and proceed to Fort William, which we reach late in the evening.

We stop a day at Fort William, and after going over the town, we start by steamer for Banavie, where we catch the canal steamer "Gondolier," and go over this magnificent route. On the way we stop and see the Falls of Foyers, which have been pronounced by Professor Wilson the most magnificent of all sights and sounds in Britain, and have been enthusiastically described by the poet Burns, and many other writers. We also saw the Monastery of St. Augustus, a fine piece of architecture.

We return to our steamer and start for Inverness, which we reach in the evening. We stay at the Station Hotel. Next morning we saw the Castle, the Cathedral, and the highlands in the river Ness, and went to the battle-field of Culloden, which has an obelisk of 1850, commemorative of the battle. In the evening we drove through the town. The next morning we inspected the markets, and other shops, and in the afternoon left for

Elgin, where I arrived in the evening. I stopped at the Golden Arms Hotel, Elgin. Next day I visited the Cathedral, Anderson's Institutions for Orphans and Aged, the Poor Asylum, or Gray's Hospital, the Lunatic Asylum, the Net Manufactory, and drove through the town, and left the next day for

Aberdeen, which I reach after four hours, and put up at Douglas Hotel. As it was a wet day I did not go out in the evening. Here I had the pleasure of meeting Mr. W. Wright, the tea merchant of Glasgow, and Mr. W. T. Clark, partner of Messrs. Charles Todd and Co., of West Hartlepool. Both were kind and jolly souls, and I had the pleasure of spending a few days with them.

The town of Aberdeen is situated on the left side of the river Dee. The building material used is granite, so that Aberdeen is called the Granite City. Many of the public edifices have the granite so worked and polished as to produce a very striking ornamental appearance. Next day I visited the following places: Tower and Town Hall, in the Castle Street, a splendid building, entirely built of granite, and which contains a number of splendid portraits of distinguished persons. I also visited the Traders' Hall in Union Street, in which there is a number of fine portraits of notable persons connected with the incorporated trades. In the banqueting room I found some chairs two hundred years old. I saw also the Hall, a fine building, to accommodate about two thousand five hundred people. A little to the right is the Blind Asylum in Huntley Street. I never saw such an institution as this before; the men and women were making baskets, coir carpets, mattresses, ropes, etc., in such an easy manner that I at first disbelieved that they were totally blind; but I was convinced by the guide that they are never permitted to enter the premises without undergoing a medical examination. There were about one hundred and fifty blind men and women working at this institution. Coming out of this street, and going a little further on, you find a bronze statue of the Prince Consort in sitting posture. From here I took a short cut and went to the Mareschal College in Broad Street. It is a famous seat of learning, and students attended from all parts of the world. In the square of the building I found an obelisk of polished granite, seventy-two feet high, erected in memory of Sir James McGregor, who held the office of Director General in the Army. Directly in front of this are the College Buildings, containing elegant and commodious class rooms, lecture hall, and an extensive museum.

I returned to my Hotel Douglas in the evening, which is situated in the Market Street, and next door to the General Post Office, a fine building; and opposite to this are the Market Buildings, which I had the pleasure of visiting the next day (Friday). An interesting spectacle was presented, as that being the market day of the week, large crowds of people resorted there for the purchasing of dairy and garden produce. The shops and stalls are well filled up in the central hall and galleries. Passing to the top of the Market Street is a fine statue of the Queen, in white marble, on a granite pedestal. I also visited the

East and West Churches and the Façade, the entrance of St. Nicholas Churchyard. From this I took a drive on the Links, a fine open space, where I found a lot of young men playing at cricket, golf, and football, and soldiers were having their evening drill. We drove round the beach, a charming drive, and reached the Bridge of Don, and left our carriage and walked up the old bridge called the Brig o' Balgownie (a Gothic arch built in the time of Robert Bruce), to which Lord Byron has dedicated a few lines. I had a charming view of the Don from this old bridge. After walking through the old town we come to the Cathedral, called Church of Old Machor, which is nearly five hundred years old. The ceiling works and well stained glass were put up lately. From here we drove up to the Imperial Crown of King's College, where we found a very large collection of books, and the marble statue of the late Mr. Jenkins, Indian Civil Service, is placed at the entrance of the library. We saw the chapel, which contains ancient carved wood pews. After going over the different rooms of this College, we drove to our hotel.

The next day I started for Ballater, which I reached the same afternoon. After spending a few hours there in visiting the Albert Memorial Hall, Francis Coutts's premises, and driving through the town, I left for Braemar the same evening. I must say the scenery between Aberdeen and Ballater is really charming. All the buildings I saw were entirely built of granite.

From Ballater I took stage coach and started for Braemar. On the road I had the pleasure of seeing the Princess Christian and her son, and a lady-in-waiting, also the royal messenger taking Her Majesty's despatches to London. On our way we saw Abergeldie Castle. We dropped mails for the Empress Eugenie, who was then living there. Half-way to Braemar stands the magnificent Balmoral Castle of Her Majesty the Queen, which we saw quite closely. It is a nice structure, consisting of two blocks, connecting wings, bartisan turrets, and a tower eighty feet high. Close to it we saw the house which was built for John Brown. Nice lawns and gardens are laid out around the castle. The Dee flows just at the foot of it, and gave a charming appearance to the castle, which is used as Her Majesty's autumnal retreat, and is maintained in strict privacy. After driving along the Dee we came to the farm belonging to Her Majesty, where a small cross is put up in memory of Her Majesty's daughter the Princess Alice. After passing Her Majesty's private bridge and road, we come to Colonel Farquharson's property, where we saw large deer forests and other fields. We here saw the huge trees blown down by the storm of the 6th March, 1883, and the hill was almost cleared of trees by the storm.

After a drive of three hours I reached Braemar in the evening, which is a charming little town, surrounded by beautiful trees and greenness. I stop at the Invercauld Arms Hotel.

The next day I took another drive to Balmoral, and the scenery was really picturesque. I spent a Sunday there, and drove to Glassalt Shiel, Blairgowrie, and the next morning I started for Aberdeen, *viâ* Ballater. At Braemar I had the pleasure of seeing Her Majesty the Queen, when passing by our hotel, Invercauld Arms, on her way to the Castle, and the Empress Eugenie, who was returning from the chapel to Abergeldie Castle.

I took train to Aberdeen, *viâ* Ballater, and, after a journey of five hours, I arrived at Aberdeen, where the weather was disagreeable, owing to rain and storms; and next day I attended the opening ceremony of Dudley Park by Princess Beatrice.

I started for Dundee, *viâ* Arbroath, which place I reached at night. I started next day for Arbroath, and visited the extensive canvas manufactory belonging to Messrs. Corsar & Sons, who very kindly showed me the whole process of making canvas, and I was greatly pleased to see the working of it. I spent the remaining portion of the day at the splendid house of this kind-hearted gentleman, Mr. W. Corsar, who very kindly showed me the town and the old Cathedral of Arbroath, and then drove up to Montrose, a most charming seaside town. After having dined at Mr. Corsar's, I left, late at night, for Dundee.

The next morning, at Dundee, I visited Mr. Joseph Barrie, the great jute dealer, and his brother, Captain Barrie, steamship owner. Mr. Barrie was kind enough to show me the Exchange and other principal buildings of Dundee.

After spending two days there, I started for Edinburgh, *viâ* Broughty Ferry. The day was not clear, and we had a pitching sea between Broughty and Tay Port. After a short run of an hour or so, I arrived at Tay Port, where a train was ready to take us to the Firth of Forth, where a steamer was waiting for us to take us to Granton.

Here we met another train, which took us to Edinburgh. I had the opportunity of seeing the Tay Bridge, which is now a complete wreck, and where a terrible accident happened, with loss of life, in the year 1879. I put up in Edinburgh at Hotel Windsor.

After staying a day in Edinburgh, I left for Manchester, which town I reached after a journey of seven hours. I here met Mr. McFee, the junior partner of Messrs. Robert Barbour Brothers, who very kindly took me round and showed me the extensive and most interesting calico-printing works of Messrs. Thomas Hoyle and Sons, of Manchester. I never before thought nor even dreamt how the printing was done, of which I saw so much this day. I was taken to a room where there was nothing but copper rollers, about seven thousand in number, each costing six pounds, with different patterns of print on them. From this to the dyeing room, and the foreman very kindly explained to me the processes, one after another, of printing the cloth. There were six hundred men employed on the works. The rapidity of little girls in folding each piece of cloth was well worth seeing, and no less interesting sights were the dyeing, bleaching, and drying of the pieces, which were marvellous in the extreme.

After visiting this, I was taken to the more extensive works of Messrs. Sharp and Murrays, the cotton-yarn and cloth manufacturers. This was a gigantic establishment, where over one thousand men and women were employed, chiefly the latter sex. The process, which was most interesting, of making cloth, from the beginning to the end was shown to me by the manager, and I was really greatly touched at the kind courtesy and urbanity that was shown to me by Mr. McFee and other gentlemen of Manchester.

I then visited the Town Hall, and the extensive shop of Messrs. Heywood and Co.'s, and then I went to my Hotel Albion, where I met my friend Elkington, nephew of General Elkington, of the Horse Guards; and after dining together, we went to see the performance at Princess's Theatre. The play was the "Bohemian Girl," most ably acted by Miss Burns.

After having spent two days in Manchester, I took leave of my friends, and left for Liverpool, which place I reached after an hour's run. I drove up to the Quays and Docks, and saw the principal buildings, and left next day, by Pullman Palace Car, for London, *viâ* Derby, and thus completed my Scotch Tour.

BRITISH TOUR.

AFTER a long absence of nearly a month in the Highlands, I returned to London on the night of the 28th *September*, 1883, at 11 p.m. I thought after such a lengthened journey I should take rest for a few days in the metropolis, but this idea was out of the question in such a bustling large city.

London fairly lays claim to be considered as the greatest city of the modern world. History does not tell us when the ancient Britons settled on the spot which now marks the site of modern London. In their days, London was but a collection of huts on a dry spot, situated in the midst of a marsh, or in a cleared part of the forest. The Britons settled down in this rude city, protecting themselves by an artificial earthwork and a ditch. After the settlement of the Romans, London commenced to grow in importance owing to the advantage of the Thames, as it afforded every facility for shipping. Merchants from different countries resorted hither from the time of the Emperor Nero. It suffered great hardships during the warfare between the Romans and Britons, and in later centuries was much ravaged and plundered by piratical hordes of Franks, Picts, Scots, Danes, and Saxons, who were attracted here, doubtless, from a knowledge of the commercial wealth of this rising city ; but, nevertheless, it marvellously and speedily recovered from these severe visitations.

During the Roman reign, London extended from the site of the present Tower of London to Ludgate, and inland from the Thames to Moorfields. The Romans constructed many roads in this city, notably Watling Street, and built an extensive wall and gates round ancient London, which in after times received the several appellations of Ludgate, Aldgate, Bishopsgate, Moorgate, Aldersgate, Newgate, etc., which are still commemorated by names of streets marking the locality. Roman London was not more than a mile in length, and about half a mile in breadth, and it is supposed that Moorgate Street, Bishopsgate, and Smithfield must have laid beyond the walled city, as Roman sepulchral remains were found here.

The Saxons did nothing towards the fortifications of London, but the great works left here by the Romans, such as temples, statuary, roads, bridges, baths, and villas were either destroyed or allowed to go to ruins, as was the case all over England. The Normans, however, did their best to fortify and embellish this famous city.

London continued steadily to increase in size and importance. In the seventeenth century, the sites of Westminster Abbey and St. Paul's Cathedral were marked by the modest originals of these magnificent buildings. William the Conqueror gave the first charter to this city. Later on, when the Magna Charta was extorted from King John, by which the ancient privileges of London were maintained, the present form of its Corporation, consisting of Mayor, Aldermen, and Common Council, may be said to have been founded. London suffered terribly from lamentable fires, famines, and pestilence, in which thousands of its inhabitants perished. During the reigns of Henry VIII. and his daughter Mary (1509—1558), London was noted for its fires lighted to consume unfortunate "heretics" at the stake, while under the subsequent calmer reign of Queen Elizabeth, the metropolis proved its patriotism by voting men, money, and ships for resisting the attack threatened by the Spanish Armada.

The streets of London were, as far as the seventeenth century, dirty, full of ruts and holes. It was not, however, till the reign of Queen Anne (1702—1714) that London commenced to show anything like its present appearance. The great storm of 1703, and the great frost from Christmas to St. Valentine's Day, 1739—40 (during which a fair was held on the frozen waters of the

Thames), are two remarkable periods in English history.

It was only during the latter half of the last century, that handsome streets and fine buildings in London commenced to rise, such as the Mansion House, the Horse Guards, Somerset House, and the Bank of England; while in the nineteenth century, the march of improvement in London has grown like magic and defies description.

In these few notes, which I wish to confine to a short description of my British Tour, it is neither my aim nor my desire to touch upon the history of this flourishing city and capital, as it were, of the modern world; but I have mentioned the short description merely to contrast the insignificant city of huts to the present enlightened London. In short, without attempting any further description of London, it may truly be said of its over-crowded population, that there are in London more Scotchmen than in Edinburgh, more Irish than in Dublin, more Jews than in Palestine, and more Roman Catholics than in Rome! and you can then consider the importance of this large commercial and stupendous city.

On the 29*th September* I had the pleasure of dining with Colonel Shadwell Clarke and many other friends at the Masonic Temple of the Holborn Restaurant.

On the next day I visited St. Paul's Cathedral

This is the largest church in England, and is a noble building. It resembles St. Peter's at Rome, but is much smaller, and is built in the form of a Latin cross. It is said to have been designed by Sir Christopher Wren. Begun in 1675, opened in 1697, completed by the same designer, and by one master mason, and under one bishop, the Right Rev. Dr. Compton. The nave is five hundred feet in length, and one hundred and eighteen feet broad, and the transept is two hundred and fifty feet long. The inner dome is two hundred and twenty-five feet in height. The outer, from the pavement to the top of the cross, is four hundred and four feet in height. The Cathedral has an extensive choir. There is a statue of Queen Anne in front of the grand entrance. The façade is approached by a flight of twenty-two marble steps; on each side of the façade there is a tower two hundred and twenty-two feet in height, with evangelical statues at the base. There is a nice peal of bells in the north tower, which I examined. The organ of the Cathedral, which is one of the best in Great Britain, is divided into two parts; one is placed on each side of the choir, and connected by mechanism under the choir flooring. There are many monuments of distinguished personages of England and India, such as Nelson, Wellington, Mountstuart Elphinstone, Sir Henry Montgomery, Laurence, Marquis Cornwallis, Dr. Samuel Johnson, and many others. I also saw the crypt, the large library, and noticed with much interest the Whispering Gallery, which is placed in the interior of the cupola, and which is reached by a flight of steps from the library, or two hundred and sixty steps from the pavement of the church. A slow whisper uttered on the wall of the gallery is distinctly echoed to the wall on the other side, a distance of one hundred and eight feet in a direct line, or one hundred and sixty feet round the semicircle.

After examining this noble edifice, containing numerous monuments, which make it a National Temple of Fame, only second to Westminster Abbey, I return quite pleased with what I have seen during the day.

The next day (30*th September*, 1883), I had the pleasure of meeting Dr. Hopkins at the Charing Cross Hotel, and, after lunching together, we went to see Whitehall, the India Office, and St. James's Park. Whitehall is named after the Royal Palace that was situated here, and for the tragic scenes enacted here we can best refer to English history. The Palace of Whitehall was destroyed by fire in 1697; the banqueting-hall is all that remains now of this remarkable structure. In the neighbourhood of Whitehall rises a large pile of buildings, containing the Government Offices, and here is situated the India Office; and I was pleased to see the handsomely furnished and decorated apartments of the building.

St. James's Park is situated to the south of St. James's Palace, which became the Royal residence after the destruction of Whitehall Palace. The park was once a marshy meadow, transformed by Henry VIII. into a deer park and riding path. Now it is one of the best parks in London—the broad avenue of handsome trees, the winding expanse of water, enlivened by the water-fowl, the suspension-bridge, and fine view of the handsome and stately buildings round it, make the place very attractive.

After visiting these, we saw Queen Anne's Mansion, near Queen Anne's Gate, and I was astonished to see gigantic buildings of thirteen stories, which Dr. Hopkins and I twice counted over; and in this large building, on the fourth floor (flat), stays the ex-Governor of Bombay, Sir Philip Wodehouse.

After visiting this locality, we went over to the extensive shop or premises of the Army and Navy Stores, in Victoria Street, where you can get anything from a pin to an anchor, and, in fact, all the articles that are to be had on the face of the earth. Hundreds of men, women, and children were assembled there to make purchases. This alone was ample proof of the extensive nature of their trade. The members only are allowed to make purchases.

After having visited these extensive shops, we went to Marlborough House, the London residence of the Prince of Wales. This residence is nicely furnished, and the lawns and gardens are tastefully laid out and well kept. From Marlborough House we went through St. James's Palace and the Beaconsfield Club, and thence to St. James's Park, and, after having spent the day with my friend, Dr. Hopkins, I returned to my hotel in the evening.

The next day (*1st October*, 1883), I visited some of the merchants in the City, and I spent the evening at the Committee's Club Dinner of the Royal Masonic Institution, Wood Green.

The following day I spent at Lee, with Mr. Warwick, whom I knew at Karachi.

On the *8th October*, I left by the evening train from St. Pancras Station to Windermere Lake-side Station, and put up at the New Hotel. I passed through Bedford and Chesterfield. After having a walk round the little village and the new Station Hotel, I took a boat and rowed on this charming lake. The length of the lake is about eleven miles, and is situated in the county of Westmoreland. The greatest extent of margin of the lake skirts Lancashire. The lake has innumerable feeders. The principal rivers which discharge their waters in this lake are the Brathy and Rothay, where they form a confluence. There are numerous islands on the lake. Windermere is the deepest of the English lakes. It is well stocked with fish. The scenery round the lake is very charming, graceful, and soft. It is entirely devoid of that wildness and natural boldness that characterizes some other lakes. There are mountains only at its head, which rise to a considerable height, whence the traveller can get a magnificent view of the grandeur of the lake. The rest of the margin is occupied by wooded eminences, which add to the richness of the scenery, which unclothed hills cannot show. There are villas and cottages amid the woods, and they impart a scenery of domestic beauty, thus enriching the landscape. The Orrest Head is the most noted of the eminences, from which a spectator gets a grand view of the lake and the surrounding mountains. I spent a day or two at this pleasant lake, and then left, next morning, for Bowness, which lies midway of the lake. The town of Bowness is very pretty, being situated on the margin of a large bay. It has a nice hotel, a church, and a handsome school-house. There are many villas round Bowness, and the walks are pretty and interesting, and you get a fine view of the lake. The lake itself presents a magnificent expanse of water, while the foreground of wood, and the background of mountains, give it a charming appearance.

Having partaken of lunch at Bowness, I left by steamer for Ambleside, lying about a mile from the head of Windermere. Ambleside is a small market town, and is built on the ruins of an ancient Roman town, and being surrounded by mountains, presents beautiful scenery, and is much resorted to in summer. The new Church of St. Mary is situated happily in the village, and contains a stained-glass window as a memorial of the poet Wordsworth. There are also many villas about Ambleside.

We took a carriage and pair from Ambleside, and drove over to the Coniston Lake, and on our way we visited the manufactory of bobbins for threads, which was worked by means of water-power, and it was the most interesting industry I ever visited. I also had the opportunity of visiting one of the slate quarries, and saw the process of slate-cutting down to the thickness of one-eighth of an inch.

The village of Coniston is situated at a distance from Coniston Water; but there is an hotel at the edge of the lake. There is a famous mountain, called the "Old Man," which abounds with slate quarries, the slate being carried down the lake in boats. There are also valuable copper mines on the mountains.

The lake itself is six miles long and about half a mile broad, and is very deep. There are two small islands on the lake. The lake is well stocked with good fish. The scenery at the upper extremity is very grand. The two mountains situated here, one of them being the "Old Man," mentioned above, contributing much grandeur to the landscape.

We then drove up to Grasmere, which is noted

for the graves of the great poets, Wordsworth and Coleridge. The charms of Grasmere have been so well described in Mrs. Hemans' Sonnet to Grasmere, and by the old poet Wordsworth, that they need no comment from me, beyond saying that the grave of this poet is marked by a plain stone, with the simple inscription of his own and his wife's name. The spot is under the majestic yews beside the gushing Rothay, encircled by green mountains; it was chosen by the poet of this region as his last resting-place, and a more suitable spot could not have been well selected.

We next visited Ullswater and Derwentwater, which are lakes of smaller sizes than Windermere, but they are very picturesque.

Ullswater is about nine miles long, and is divided by the mountains into three reaches, as they are called here. The extreme width is about three-quarters of a mile. There are few islands on the lake, and in the neighbourhood there are many nooks and recesses in the dells and by the lake, decked with wild flowers, and the sail on the lake is very pleasant.

The grandeur of Derwentwater is more imposing. In form it is an oval, about three miles in length, and about one and a half miles in breadth, running into an amphitheatre of mountains, that are very rugged, but not very high, craggy, and broken into splinters and peaked, and there are narrow valleys, giving a view of the rocks rising beyond. The margin of the lake is covered with green pastures, and is, at places, adorned with woody eminences; and the sight of a white cottage peeping from among them gives a lively view to the scenery. The aspect is heightened when, in calm weather, the waters reflect the whole picture, as the water is very clear, and you can discern objects at fifteen to twenty feet below its clear surface. As the lake is small, clean, and charming beyond measure, many travellers give preference to Derwentwater than to the rugged mountain scenery of the Highlands. It must be noted that St. Herbert's Isle is situated in the middle of the lake. It takes its name from the holy hermit who dwelt here, and the remains of the hermitage are yet visible. There is a natural phenomenon worthy of notice in these waters, what is termed the "Floating Island," which rises at irregular intervals in a few years from the bottom to the surface; its extent varies in different years.

We returned late to our hotel, the Salutation at Ambleside, and as I had to see one of my friends off to India from London, I left for the latter place the same night, arriving in London the next morning. Having fulfilled this duty, I started back again to resume my travels, and I arrived the next morning at Bradford, which is the seat of stuff and woollen yarns. There are coal and iron works in its vicinity. The city contains numerous churches, a town-hall, theatre, public buildings, and charitable institutions.

While at Bradford, I visited St. George's Hall, and there saw a piece acted, called "Adamless Eden." In this, none but young ladies were acting, even in the orchestra the music was played by young girls. This was really a novel sight, and very amusing. I afterwards visited the town, which is full of cotton manufactories. I was greatly pleased to see one of the largest warehouses in Bradford of cotton goods belonging to A. and T. Henry and Co., and saw thousands of pieces of all kinds of woollen goods of different sorts, colours, and sizes, and it was very interesting to notice the different shades of colour given to cotton and woollen goods, which, in many respects, appeared as silk. The managing partner of this firm, Mr. Mitchell, who was Mayor of Bradford a year before, asked me to dine with him, and assist him to receive the members of the Cloth-maker's Association from London, that were coming to Bradford the same evening, but having so many other previous engagements, I had to decline this kind invite of Mr. Mitchell with many thanks, and after having inspected the Technical School, comprising drawing, painting, sketching, and classics, and of which Mr. Mitchell was the president and promoter, I left quite pleased with what I had seen in this manufacturing town. Left the same day for Saltaire.

This charming little town belongs to Sir Titus

Salt, Baronet, situated on the river Aire, from which it derives its name, viz., Salt Aire. No sooner arrived at the station, we were taken to the most splendidly built spinning and weaving wool manufactory of Sir Titus Salt, Bart., Son, and Co., situated about twenty yards from the station, where I was introduced to the chief partner, Mr. Titus Salt, also Messrs. Stead, Clove, and Moore. The most gigantic piece of machinery and working of the great factory were shown to me. I was first shown round the place where the bales of wool were unpacked and washed. From there we were shown where it was dried and combed. After this we were shown where the web was formed, and then the threads, and at last we were ushered in a huge room where there were one thousand looms working in full swing, making woollen cloths of all sizes and description. I have never been over such a gigantic woollen manufactory where there were one thousand looms, and where there were five thousand men, women, and children at work. The huge factory was worked by means of three engines, two of which were five hundred horse power each, with eleven boilers, consuming forty tons of coal daily. I was particularly asked to see the people coming out of the factory at 12.30, when it was dinner time. I was pleased to see some thousands of persons pouring forth from the gate in their working garments, and to see one great mass of moving objects was interesting.

I was then shown round the Institute and Hospital, established by Sir Titus Salt for the recreation and comfort of the people of Saltaire, numbering about five thousand five hundred in number. The Institution is a very solid and handsome building, and provided with all sorts of comforts and recreations. The Hospital was replete with all medicines and equipments. I have the satisfaction to say, that in token of my visit to this most interesting town of Saltaire, where I spent some hours in witnessing most interesting sights, I allowed my name to be associated in this Institute by becoming a life member. After having seen these objects, Mr. Titus Salt requested me to lunch with him, which I did with pleasure, and here I was introduced to some of the partners of the firm, who presented me with a plan of the mill and a photograph of the Institute.

I then left for Leeds. This is the principal seat of woollen manufacture in England. It stands on the river Aire. There are numerous churches and commercial buildings, Stock Exchange, a new Town Hall, opened by the Queen in 1858, theatre, schools, charitable buildings, baths, and military barracks. It is most noted for its cloth halls, where extensive sales of woollen cloths take place. There are also iron foundries, chemical works, and soap factories, as also markets for sale of leather goods. I was met at Leeds by Mr. Elliott of the Midland Railway, who had very kindly arranged for me to visit the extensive iron manufactory of the Monk Bridge Iron Company, belonging to Messrs. Kitson and Co. I never saw such an extensive manufactory of heavy iron works before in my life, such as railway engines, boilers, shafts, etc., the rolling of metal, the casting, melting, hammering, polishing, and some fifty other processes were shown to me in this factory, each of them very interesting and instructive, that for a time I was bewildered; to see gigantic iron works executed in front of me, the lifting and fixing of the huge machinery, were also sights worth seeing. Here were locomotive engines getting ready for the Great Indian Peninsular Railway and Indus Valley State Railway, also for the Great Western Railway of England.

After having gone through these works of Kitson's, where we met the Honourable Mr. Pearson, partner of Mr. Kitson, we left the factory greatly pleased.

After this we visited the factory of Messrs. Fowler and Co., of Leeds, the greatest agricultural implement manufacturers in the world. The factory was fitted up with electric light, so at night you can see the works as if done in broad daylight. I was here again thunderstruck to see the castings of huge iron works. How the liquid mass of iron was coming forth from a large spout in great volumes, and the way the huge vats of this liquid metal poured in different moulds, was a sight worth seeing, highly interesting and instructive. There were two thousand men in their employ. Some hundreds of ploughing, shearing machines, locomotives, etc., were ready to be shipped off to different parts of the world; and some thousands of other small agricultural implements were seen stacked in their extensive premises all ready to be shipped off. I had the satisfaction to see at these two places, viz., Bradford and Leeds, many articles got up for the Calcutta Exhibition, viz., from Bradford, a selection of cotton, woollen, and silken goods; from Manningham, velvet. All these were shown to me in the technical school at Bradford. From Messrs. Kitson's, at Leeds, there were two railway engines, three self-smoke-consuming train engines; and from Messrs. Fowler and Co., three ploughing and shearing machines were ready to be exhibited at Calcutta, and thence they were to be sent on to Australia.

After having seen these principal iron manufactories of Leeds, I went out to see the town, which was then gaily decorated with flags and evergreens, as the royal guests, the Duke and Duchess of Albany, had arrived here to open the bazaar and attend the musical festival, which was got up on a grand scale. They left the same day for Huddersfield, and I turned my course towards Nottingham.

Nottingham is noted for its lace manufacture, and

is a place of ancient origin, and figured much in history as the scene of many a sanguinary struggle; but the modern improvements have distinguished this city as being well built, clean, and healthy.

I was met here by Mr. Holt, who had very kindly arranged to show me the extensive manufactory of hosiery belonging to Messrs. Morley. It was here I saw for the first time in my life how socks, stockings, underskirts, under-drawers, etc., both of wool, cotton, and silk, were manufactured. It was really very interesting. There were about twelve hundred people, chiefly girls, employed at this establishment. I was shown round the whole manufactory by the manager, and I was quite astonished when I was taken to the cutting department to learn that four girls cut every year twenty thousand pieces as under-drawers only. The knitting by machinery was very fine and interesting.

From this place we were taken to Messrs. Cutt's Lace Manufactory. It is very difficult for me to describe how this work is accomplished. I was quite surprised to see huge iron machines turn out so fine an article as cotton and silk lace, some of them not even three-quarters of an inch in width. Door, window, and mosquito curtains, of all sizes, shapes, and qualities, were made here, and the working of it was a curiosity to me. The filling up of threads in brass bobbins, and other processes, were all shown to me, and to describe all would occupy an amount of time and space which I have not at my disposal for the present.

From Messrs. Cutt's we went over to the extensive lace warehouse belonging to Messrs. Adam and Co. Here I was taken to the room where there were some thousands bales of lace stacked as they were received from the factories. The processes of bleaching, rolling, packing, etc., were shown to me. About one thousand girls are employed to sort the lace, sew, stitch, and frill the laces, after different styles and fashions. Some thousands of different cotton and silk laces, some hundreds of door, window, and mosquito curtains, chair and pillow covers, were shown to me, and I was simply charmed to see the exquisite workmanship. Some of their curtains and antimacassars were exhibited at the International Exhibition of 1862. I was greatly amused to see the girls' bonnets and caps that were made here, also frills of some hundred sorts turned out by machinery, which was very interesting. It took us nearly five hours to go through this extensive warehouse. I left the premises after having signed my name as a visitor, and after having received a sketch of their building, etc., we went to see the Nottingham Castle. I should not omit to mention that in Messrs. Adam's premises there is a chapel situated within the grounds of their extensive establishment, where a paid clergyman attends every morning to hold a service for one hour before the men begin their work, and it is a standing rule that no men should go to work unless they attend Divine service every morning.

Nottingham Castle is now converted into a Fine Art Museum, which we saw. The gardens are nicely laid out. After taking a view of the town from the top of this castle, which is very picturesque, and after having seen the Picture Gallery, we went round the city, where I visited a few of my friends, and returned to my hotel in the evening. While visiting the city, I drove right up to the splendid iron bridge built over the Trent, from whence you could see a charming scenery round the town.

After dinner, I left for Leicester, which place I reached in about two hours. An annual fair, called the Onion Fair, was going on then. It was a great sight, and I never before witnessed a country fair like this. It was held just in front of my hotel. Some hundred thousand persons had assembled to witness it, and as it was a fine Saturday evening, some thousands had come from the adjacent towns to spend the Saturday night and Sunday. All sorts of gaieties were performed. There were numberless shops of sweets and refreshment stalls erected ; there were merry-go-rounds, theatricals, circus, menagerie, shows, etc., all in full swing ; and I visited each and every pavilion which contained funny things, one way or the other. The next morning (Sunday), I took a cab and drove through the town, and went to Abbey Park, which was only opened a few years ago by the Princess of Wales. I here saw beautiful beds of flowers, tastefully laid out, and some artificial lakes. The principal streets of Leicester are the Queen's and the Duke streets, where beautiful houses are to be seen. After visiting the statue of the Duke of Rutland, which is cast in full size, I returned to my hotel. Leicester is the capital of the county of Leicestershire, and is situated on the river Soar, which is crossed by four bridges. The principal manufacture is woollen hosiery. There are many churches, an excellent theatre, chamber of commerce, public library and museum, and numerous societies and schools.

After taking dinner at my hotel, I left for Birmingham the same evening, at which place I arrived after a quick run of two hours. I stayed at the Midland Hotel. Birmingham is one of the principal manufacturing towns of England, and is noted all over the world for its extensive manufactures of every kind of iron, brass, steel, and electro-plate ; its buttons, toys, jewellery, pins, steel pens, glass, cutlery, and different other trades. The town is comparatively of modern origin. In 1676 it was but a market town, and it has solely risen by the growth of its industries ; and Edmund Burke has justly pronounced Birmingham to be the "toy-shop of the world." It is also famous for its Mint, which coins money for the United Kingdom, Turkey, China, Hayti, Sarawak, Tuscany, Canada, Chili, Italy, and other countries.

The next morning, I met Mr. Holmes, who had kindly arranged to show me round the principal manufacturing places of Birmingham, which, as I have said above, is known far and wide for its works. The first manufactory we visited was the pin-making. I was never so much surprised as on seeing this small object made by means of huge machinery. Mr. Jowett, the managing partner, was, indeed, kind enough to go with us through his works, and explained minutely the process of pin making. I was greatly interested to see the coil of wire cut into small bits, tapped, and ends sharpened, and found ready-made pins at the end. All this process was done by one machine, completing the different stages at the same time. This is really very interesting. The pins are then taken to a room where there are copper vats full of boiling water, with tin in them. The pins are thrown into these, and well stirred till they are tinned, and after going through this process they are removed and put into wooden casks filled with sawdust, and turned well till they are polished, and all the oily substance is well removed. After this process, they are carried to the packers, who are young girls. These pins are filled in a box, under which are iron frames with holes in them, and the paper is driven in from one way, and the pins begin sticking on it. After the pins are stuck on the papers, they go to the packers, who tie and make into bundles. All these were explained to me, from a piece of wire till it was turned into a fine packet of pins. I should not omit to mention, that in one pound of brass wire twenty-four thousand pins of smallest size were turned out, and in one minute they can make one hundred and eighty. The weekly consumption of brass wire was sixty hundred weight, and Messrs. Jarratt and Rainsford had in their employ about five hundred men and girls. Before leaving the premises, Mr. Jarratt presented me with a packet of pins which were made in my presence, and I accepted the packet with many thanks.

We next went to see another interesting manufactory, that of steel pen making, belonging to Messrs. Gillott and Co. The forewoman received us very kindly, and asked another young lady to take us round and explain the steel pen making, which the young lady did in a masterly way. We were first shown the steel plates, which were rolled of exact thickness. After that the plates were cut in small strips, and each strip was handed over to young girls, who had a punching machine near them; and then the small strips of steel were cut into small pieces, in length of nibs, or pens, turned half round. These small nibs or pens, were removed to another room, where they were split, and holes bored through them. After this they were given into the hands of girls to be sharpened, which was done very cleverly, and each end of the nib, or steel pen, had to go through the grinding process. From this the pens had to be polished and hardened, which was done in other rooms. After going through all these processes, the pens were removed to the packers, where some hundred girls were seen making small boxes from cardboard. In these boxes twelve dozens were filled and packed into bundles. All this was really very interesting. I signed the visitors' book, and left the premises greatly pleased.

From this place I went over to the extensive manufactory of Messrs. Elkington and Co., the great silversmiths and electro-platers, and bronze founders. I was quite astonished to see their show-rooms, which were full of silver-plate ware, all very handsomely and richly carved, some of the articles costing from fifty to two thousand pounds. After having signed the visitors' book, a young lady very kindly took us round the extensive works, and showed us the process of making, carving, soldering, electro-plating, and different other processes of silver works. I was greatly surprised to see a plate that was getting ready for the Kensington Museum, which will cost, when ready, three thousand pounds; men have been working on it three years, and they are expected to complete the chasing work by the end of the present year (1883). I was also greatly interested to see the tea, coffee, and other sets; also spoons, forks, dishes, and some thousand other articles, all interesting and instructive. I am sorry I cannot describe here more fully the processes of making these articles as shown and explained to me.

From this we returned to Queen's Hotel, and after having luncheon, we went to Handsworth by railway train, to see the great works of Messrs. Tangye Brothers, a name known throughout the world for their works. I was here introduced to Mr. Howse, the private secretary of Mr. Richard Tangye, who very kindly asked one of the foremen of the works to show us the great manufactory. I must say that I never came across such gigantic buildings, spread over some acres of land. The first shop we were shown was where patent crank shafts were made; then the cutting, boring, polishing, and different other shops. Then we were conducted where the boilers were made and rivetted. The process was extremely interesting. The huge rivetting work was done without the least noise, and a rivet, as much as six inches in length and one and a quarter inches in thickness, was drawn and tapped like a piece of cotton, or some such soft object. Then we were conducted and shown round where railway carriage-springs, wheels, and tyres were rolled, and the hundred-ton steam-hammer working. We were also conducted to the blasting-furnace. Here I saw the iron melted in liquid state, and come forth in large columns; every vat filled with this liquid iron weighed nearly forty to fifty tons. The process of filling and emptying this vat was done through machinery and by travelling crane moved on rails or beams. From here we went over to the brass-turning shops, where different engines are made. All these processes were as interesting as could be imagined. I saw the making of jack-screws of some five different descriptions and sizes. I was shown the jack-screw that could lift up two hundred tons of weight, and which was used to float the Great Eastern steamer when she was first launched in water. There are five thousand men employed by the firm, and nearly one hundred tons of coal are burned to keep the factory going every day. I saw some of the Great Indian Peninsular Railway engines getting ready for Bombay. After seeing the works all over for nearly five hours, we returned to Birmingham by rail.

The next day we visited the barracks of the Birmingham Fire Brigade, where I was met by an Alderman of Birmingham, who very kindly showed me the premises. After seeing this, Mr. Alderman Elloway very kindly asked me if I was willing to see the turn-out of the Brigade, which of course I did very much like to see; and I was never so much surprised as I was on that evening, when I found the Brigade turn out, with their horses in carriage, perfectly equipped for fire service, in less than forty-two seconds. Before the fire-alarm was given, the Alderman particularly requested me to take the time, and we all (three of us) took it, and saw the turn out as I said before, and they started off at once on their way in less than forty-two seconds. I was really greatly interested, and admired the quickness and activity of the men, and the way they did their duty. After my signing the visitors' book, the secretary presented me with two copies of the rules and regulations and the formation of the corps. I left the barracks with the Alderman to the Norfolk Hotel, where we had refreshments, and returned to my Midland Hotel.

The next morning we visited the Free Library and Corporation House of Birmingham. These are elaborately-built structures. Then we visited the monument erected to Mr. Chamberlain, M.P. for Birmingham. After this, we drove through Corporation Street and Coleman Road, the two splendid streets of Birmingham, where magnificent buildings have lately been erected, and a spot worth visiting. From here we went to the great manufactory of F. and C. Osler, where we were received by Mr. F. Osler, who showed us round his extensive manufactory of chandeliers, lamps, and table glasses of all description. I was simply surprised to see a magnificent bedstead, made entirely from cut glass, and the work elaborately finished; costing them upwards of one thousand pounds, and intended to be exhibited at the Calcutta Exhibition. We were then shown how the glasses were cut and polished, and some twenty different processes were explained to us, which were very interesting. I was also extremely pleased to see their stock of glassware, which was very elegantly got up. From here we went over to the glass blasting factory. I was ushered here by the foreman into an extensive room where there were some fifty persons blowing ; the sand, acids, and other ingredients were shown to me that formed crystal glass. I saw the huge furnace which contained the vat full of liquid glass ; then the process of blowing, and then how the articles were formed and shaped. I was really greatly pleased to note the exactness of glassware manufacture. I was highly satisfied with what I had seen here, and left for the Brass and Iron Tube Works of Messrs. J. Booth and Co.

This was again an interesting place of work to witness : large pieces of brass metal were rolled under huge machinery till they attained the required thickness. After that the pieces had to go through a round hole driven by machine, and having been thus twisted, or got the round shape, it was handed over to girls to be soldered or riveted. When soldered, the tubes were filed off, and then turned on lathes to be cleaned, and a coat of varnish was applied to attain its perfection. Besides these boiler tubes, there were many other fancy tubes shown to me, and the way they were worked out was very interesting. These tubes were chiefly used for bedstead and other articles.

After having acquired a short knowledge of this tube making, we went over to see the great gun manufactory of the world-known firm of Messrs. Isaak Hollis and Sons. The manager received us at the office and conducted us to the workshop. I do not for a moment think, that out of one hundred men, ninety-nine know how a gun, pistol, or rifle is made. I was quite surprised to see the different parts of guns manufactured from common English iron. Common, because it is originally so, but after having gone through so many different processes, and which were very kindly and explicitly shown to me by each of the foremen of different sections of this intricate work. I was simply surprised when I knew all this. The iron from which the barrel is made is a piece of iron of about two feet to three feet long, one inch broad, and about one-eighth inch to a quarter inch thick ; it is turned or coiled. After being coiled, it is made red-hot, and then well hammered till it becomes one solid mass of tube. Then it is sent on to the factory to be well turned and ground, then the spring, and other minor, but most intricate parts, are made.

To describe all would require some days, and a thorough professional knowledge, which I have not. But the other processes of stock making, polishing, carving, and the last finishing touch to this deadly weapon are so interesting, that I warmly thanked the manager for the calm manner he explained to me all and every part of the gun making. As I had invited the Alderman to dine with me, I had to hasten my departure from this factory, and arrived at my hotel, where I had the pleasure of meeting my guest. After dining, we went over to see the gas and sewage works belonging to the Corporation of the City of Birmingham, the Alderman having kindly promised to show and explain these important matters more fully; and thus I concluded my visit to Birmingham, which I consider one of the greatest manufacturing towns of the world.

After having spent three days in Birmingham, I left for Sheffield *viâ* Derby, which I reached after a run of one and a half hours. I was here met by Mr. James Holt, who had very kindly managed about my seeing many interesting sights in Sheffield.

This celebrated manufacturing town derives its name from its situation on the river Sheaff, or (Sheff), which unites with the river Don. This town is noted throughout the world, from a very early period, for its cutlery manufactures. Here are situated many manufactories for all kinds of iron and steel goods, plated ware, metallic instruments, and type foundries. There is a bronze statue to Ebenezer Elliott, "The Corn Law Rhymer," opposite the post office. There are numerous public buildings and churches of all denominations, and Sheffield may fairly be said to be the "Steel Metropolis" of England or of the United Kingdom.

The first place we visited in Sheffield was the great armour plate and Atlas steel manufactory of Sir James Brown and Co. I was here quite astonished to see the gigantic machinery working. I was quite bewildered to see the blasting furnace; although it was broad day-light, yet the furnace had more powerful glare than that of the sun. I could not possibly look at the furnace, and to behold the stream of liquid iron pouring out in tremendous quantity, was a sight indescribable; then the huge iron plate, weighing about forty tons, that was got ready red hot, to receive the contents of this vat, was also a sight worth seeing. To lift a plate weighing forty tons, twenty-two inches thick, and about twelve feet long, required a huge and strong machinery, but the work was accomplished in such an easy and plain style as if to lift a little baby in a man's arm. The whole thing was accomplished in fifteen minutes, and the huge machinery was working like tame animals. After having thus acquired a vivid notion of casting of armour plates for Her Majesty's steam frigates, we went to see how they were rolled, cut, and planed, bored, and other different processes, which were one and all interesting and worth seeing. After this we went to the department where tyres for wheels were made, and saw some that were getting ready for the B. B. and C. I. Railway of India, and saw springs for railway carriages. The process was shown and explained to us by the foreman in charge in a very explicit manner. After this we went and saw the casting of steel ingots, which was another grand sight. Here we were offered goggles of neutral tint colour to wear, in order to protect our eyes from the burning heat, and with these we saw the glare of the furnace. The process of casting steel could be discerned better by the wear of the goggles. After this we were shown the original state of iron as dug out from mines, mixed with earth, and the way it was melted and turned into pig iron, which was another interesting sight. We spent five hours in this gigantic iron manufactory of Sir J. Brown, where five thousand men were employed at these huge works. I was not so surprised at the machines as I was at this gigantic manufactory, and at the work there turned out by men in a way so creditable to the employers.

From this place we went to the edge tool works of Spear and Jackson, and I was greatly pleased to see the shovels, spades, rakes, gouges of all sizes, hammers of all sorts and sizes, and different other tools, of which I have so much to do in my line, and I was the more interested when I was taken to the file-making shop of all sorts and sizes. Some thousands of files must have passed through my hands, but I never for a moment thought how they were manufactured, till I saw the whole process, from beginning to end, done in front of my eyes, and as easy as you can imagine. There were seven hundred men employed in this factory.

After this I went to see the extensive cutlery works of Messrs. Joseph Rogers and Sons, a household Indian word for cutlery. Nobody in India would think of taking articles of any other manufacturer but of Rogers. His name is known throughout the length and breadth of the world, but very few can go and see how the very articles that they use daily are manufactured. I was first ushered to the show room, where a lady received us, and showed us what she had in the room, and I was greatly delighted to see some of the tiniest little knives, scissors, say a quarter of an inch long, and about one-sixth inch thick, all fixed with blades and made in same shape as the ordinary pocket or large knives and scissors. Then to this contrast we were shown a piece of cutlery containing three hundred and sixty blades, each blade represents different towns, and some beautiful engraving on it ; but I was astonished to see a huge piece of cutlery containing one thousand eight hundred and eighty blades, which had received three gold medals in different exhibitions. Nobody would believe me if I were to say that I saw a piece containing one thousand eight hundred and eighty blades, but it is a fact, which could be easily seen in this show room. After having seen some hundreds of different other articles, we were shown round their factory, where one thousand eight hundred men were working. I was greatly pleased to see the grinding shops, where some thousands of tools were got ready for the market.

After having seen all different processes for three hours, we left the place, greatly satisfied, for the huge silver and electro-plate manufactory of James Dixon and Co. Here there were eight hundred men and women employed, and the process was similar to that I had seen at Elkington's manufactory in Birmingham, which is, however, on a much larger scale. Having seen these factories, I drove round the town, which is not so clean as Birmingham or Manchester. I drove over to the rivers Don and Sheaf, and thus completed my sight-seeing in Sheffield.

I started next day for Shorncliffe, to visit the coal-mine of Messrs. Newton, Chambers, and Co., which is about eighteen hundred feet deep. Here I was very kindly received by Mr. Hodgson and Mr. Chambers, junior. At first we were shown the plan, on which are all the different sections of the mines in work. Then we were taken to the lamp-room. There the use of Davy's Safety Lamps was explained to us. Then we were conducted to the fan-room, where the air was carried to the coal-mine by means of machinery. After this we were requested to take our hats and coats off, as we had to descend the pit, and then a lamp, a stick, and a hat were provided us. We went to the cage, and in the twinkling of an eye we were safely landed at the bottom of the pit. It took thirty-two seconds to descend. Then we were shown round the seam which they were now working. We went nearly a mile and a half inside, and saw the whole process minutely. There were single and double lines of rail laid to convey the coal to the mouth of the pit, and to carry the trucks; there were about one hundred horses and four hundred men employed in the mine. The stables for horses were well arranged.

After having been in the mine for four hours, we were hauled up; our faces and bodies were full of coal-dust, and we looked more like colliers than ordinary travellers. We were met at the office, which is only a few yards from the coal-pit, by Mr. Chambers, the managing partner of Messrs. Newton and Chambers, who showed us every kindness and courtesy; and after a good wash, he drove us to Haylands, where he had luncheon ready for us, of which we heartily partook, and left again for Sheffield. From there I took the train in the evening for Liverpool, which place I reached at midnight, and thus completed my tour in South Yorkshire.

I completed my tour in South Yorkshire on the

night of the 18th of October, and after this I thought of taking a tour through Ireland; but before doing so, I visited some more of the English towns, and the first one I visited was Woolwich, the great military station for Artillery.

I went to Woolwich by one of the Thames steamers, and visited the training ship, "Warspite." After driving through the town, I visited the great Arsenal of England and the Dockyard, which were very interesting indeed. After spending one day in Woolwich, I returned, *viâ* the Tower Hill Station of the Underground Railway to Charing Cross Station.

The next day I had the pleasure of meeting Sir W. P. Andrew, the Chairman of the S. P. and D. Railway, and the Director of the B. I. S. N. Company, who very kindly asked me over to his house to lunch with him, and there I met Mr. Norman, his able secretary, and Mr. Duncan Andrew, his amiable nephew. I had introductions to these gentlemen, through Mr. Campbell.

After spending the day with these gentlemen, I left, next day, for Tilbury, to see my friend, Mr. Campbell, off to Karachi. When I had wished him "Good-bye," I visited the famous town of Gravesend, which is a nice little shipping port. After driving through the town and the Italian Gardens, I spent the remainder of the evening at the Clarendon Hotel, and returned late to my hotel in London.

The next day I called on my reverend friend, Mr. Ffinch, at Northfleet, where I visited the College, and spent the evening at Gravesend, and returned to London the same evening.

IRISH TOUR.

I STARTED from St. Pancras Station for my tour in Ireland, and I reached Barrow-in-Furness *viâ* Leeds the same night, and crossed the Irish Channel in the fine steamer "Londonderry," arriving in Belfast early next morning.

After taking breakfast at the Queen's Hotel, I visited the principal places of Belfast; the Donegal Street and Place, and the buildings situated on them are very pretty. The whole town stands upon the property of the Marquis of Donegal, and is situated on the river Logan. The general appearance of the town is clean, thrifty, and business-like, and much resembles Manchester and Glasgow, but without the smoke or dirt of either.

I visited the Ulster and Belfast Banks, the two most handsome and largest buildings of Belfast; also the new Custom House, Museum, and Royal Academical Institution. I also paid a visit to the great ropemakers, Messrs. Morrow, Miskelly, and Co. The manager of the company received me very kindly, and after seeing the principal sights of Belfast, I started the next day for Portrush *via* Antrim and Coleraine. The scenery between Belfast and Portrush is very pretty, and especially between Coleraine, Port Stewart, and Portrush, is simply charming.

On arriving at Portrush I took my breakfast at the Northern Counties Railway Station Hotel, and started immediately in a cab for the Giant's Causeway *via* Bushmills, which is eight miles distant. On arriving at the Causeway Hotel I discharged my cab, and took a boat and four men and pulled out to sea, where we had a splendid view of the rock. To describe this Nature's beauty is really very difficult. The majority of these rocks are composed of perpendicular columns, some five, some six sided; and though separate, fitting so closely together as to exclude in some places even a sheet of paper. There are about forty thousand columns of this work of Nature, all beautifully cut and polished, and formed of such neat pieces, so exactly fitted to each other, and so closely supported, that we might fancy we had before us the work of ingenious human artificers.

After rowing for about one and a half miles we come to the Portcoon Cave, which is more than six hundred feet deep. It possesses no other interest beyond being a cave where the echo of a musical instrument is said to be very grand. We now land at the great Causeway and inspected the Amphitheatre, which is certainly the best in the world, that in Rome not excepted. No architect could shape better the half circle, the cliff sloping at precisely the same angle all round to the centre. The row of the pillars, the benches, and the enclosure of the water beneath by a circle of boulder stones, like the limits of the arena, present a scene of grandeur and admiration of Nature's art. We also inspected the Giant's Chimney Tops, which are three isolated pillars standing on the promontory; the well, etc. We went over the hill and met our carriage near the hotel. I never saw such a beautiful sight before. I again drove through Bushmill and arrived at my hotel.

I left the next day for Londonderry, which place I reached after a run of four hours. Londonderry is situated on the river Foyle; the town is fortified with walls which are about twenty-one feet in thickness, and which are still preserved as a promenade. The appearance of the town from the opposite side of the river is very picturesque, and an elegant iron bridge is constructed across the river, and a cathedral erected on the summit of the hill which is well worth visiting; also the monument raised in 1828 to the memory of the Rev. George Walker. The town has a good public hall, and on the day I visited this place a disturbance was going on, owing to some party feelings. The Lord Mayor of Dublin had come to this place to give a lecture; the subject was "Public Franchise." The

Nationalists did not like the idea of the lecture being delivered by the Lord Mayor, and I was afterwards informed that the quarrel ended in a free fight, and the military were called out to quell the riot.

After spending a day at Derry, I started for the famous city of Dublin, the capital of Ireland. On my way to Dublin I visited the military towns of Inniskillen and Tipperary, where there was nothing much to be seen but huge barracks for soldiers. I arrived in Dublin the next day, and stayed at Morrison's Hotel. I never for a moment expected that the capital town of Ireland was so clean and beautifully built, for I had a very poor opinion about cleanliness of the men, and I never found so lazy and dirty a set of people as the Irish; but Dublin had changed my opinion altogether—buildings so clean and fine, and people looked smart and busy. The following places of interest were visited by me :—

The Bank of Ireland, in College Green, which was in former times used as a Parliament House. After visiting the interior arrangements of the building, the most interesting object I witnessed was the printing of bank notes, which was really very skilfully done.

The Trinity College, which stands just opposite to my Hotel Morrison, consists of spacious courtyards, dining-hall, library, geological museum, and lecture rooms. In College Green stands the statue of King William III.

The Castle of Dublin is a huge white structure of stone, with a fine, spacious courtyard. There are several Government Offices of the State, and the Viceregal party spends winter at the Castle. In the Castle is the Viceregal Chapel, some private apartments, portrait chamber, and private drawing-rooms.

The General Post-Office, Nelson's Monument, and Custom House are buildings really well worth visiting. There is, also, on this side of the river, a most magnificent block of buildings, called the Four Courts—viz., the Queen's Bench, Chancery, Exchequer, and Common Pleas, in this one building. I also visited St. Stephen's Green, a most charming park, situated in the heart of the city, very nicely kept up.

I had also the pleasure of visiting the most extensive premises of Sir Arthur Guinness, the great brewer of the world; saw thousands of stout casks piled up, railway trucks, horse vans, and so many vehicles of different sorts were employed to remove the gigantic stock of stout that was ready to be shipped to different parts of the world, that it was a sight worth seeing.

The last thing I saw in Dublin was the Phœnix Park, a place where the most atrocious murders of the late Lord Cavendish and Mr. Burke were committed. I took a coach and drove round that park, which covers an area of nearly one thousand eight hundred acres, and is well planted with trees. On one side of the park is the Wellington Testimonial, erected in 1817 by the townspeople, at a cost of twenty thousand pounds. In the same park are the Carlyle Memorial Statue, Military Hospital, Constabulary Barracks, and the Zoological Gardens; also, the summer residence of the Viceroy, called the Viceregal Lodge. I was, indeed, greatly pained when I was shown the very spot where the two gentlemen were stabbed to death, and the route taken by the culprits after committing this horrible deed. Up to this date there is nothing marked or erected over the spot to commemorate this horrible deed. I felt bitterly for these gentlemen who fell under the assassin's hand. I had some conversation with the coachman who drove me to the Phœnix Park, who feelingly spoke, and said that this horrid deed has brought an everlasting disgrace—in fact, a crushing blow—on Ireland. He again bitterly complained that poor Lord Cavendish was murdered without any cause; on the contrary, he was much liked by the people, and they all deeply felt his loss.

After spending two days in Dublin, I went to Blackrock, near Dublin, to pay a visit to my old friend, Mr. T. G. Newnham, so well known in Scinde. After spending some pleasant hours with him, I returned to Dublin, and left, the next day, for the Lakes of Killarney, *viâ* Dundalk and Drogheda. I stayed at Killarney at the Railway Station Hotel, which was very comfortable. The next morning we formed a party, and drove up to the Lakes of Killarney, through Muckross, the property of Mr. Herbert, M.P. The scenery on the banks of the middle lake is simply charming, the flower-beds and other trees are thickly planted, and the sight I saw was magnificent, and shall never be forgotten. It is really a source of great pity that up to this time no small steamers are allowed to run on any of these lakes. After going as far as the Gap of Dunloe, we discharged our cab, and took a boat and rowed round the upper and middle lake, and thus spent a day in great enjoyment. Although the Lakes of Killarney are of less extent, and devoid of that sublimity attaching to the lochs of Scotland, they possess some remarkable features, such as the dense woods that surround them, the imposing contours of the mountains, the numberless islands, and their luxuriant vegetation. The striking scenery is of the plant arbutus, which freely grows here; its fresh green tints contrast so well with the grey rocks among which it flourishes. These celebrated lakes of Ireland are divided into three parts—the Upper Lake, the Muckross Torc, or Middle Lake, and Lough Leane, or the Lower Lake.

The Upper Lough is two and a half miles by three-quarters, covering an area of four hundred and thirty acres, and contains about twelve small islands. Though small in proportion, this lake is admitted to be the best of the three, on account of the wild, rocky shores which encompass it on every side. The landscape is one of grandeur, as the softer beauties of wood and water are contrasted with the reality of mountain scenery that delights the eye and gratifies the imagination of the visitor.

Muckross Torc, or Middle Lake. This lake has an area of six hundred and eighty acres. It contains two principal islands, which are well wooded, and the scenery is very pleasant.

Lough Leane, or the Lower Lake, contains about five thousand acres, and is the largest lake. There are upwards of thirty islands, few exceeding an area of about one acre. The chief beauty of this lake consists in the wide, placid surface of the water, and the mountains which form its barriers on the south and west. There are innumerable nooks of great beauty in the bays and inlets; the verdant shores, and the richly-clothed islands of Innisfallen and Ross, and the mirror-like surface of the lake, gives to the scenery of this lake a magnificent grandeur. What Loch Katrine is to Scotland, Lough Leane is to Ireland, though the latter cannot compare to the former in the romantic grandeur of scenery.

I returned to my hotel late in the evening, and left the next day for Waterford, a small sea-port town. From there I started by the steamer "Limerick," for Milford Haven, and after steaming for nearly twelve hours, we reached the last port, where we met a heavy gale and strong rain—in fact, very disagreeable weather.

Spending half a day at Milford, I started for London, *viâ* Gloucester. The scenery I saw between St. Fagan, Newnham, and Gloucester was simply indescribable. I was charmed with it, and the beautiful iron bridge on the Severn was another grand sight to witness. On my way I visited the famous town of Cardiff, remained there for some hours, and left for London; and thus completed my tour from North to South of Ireland.

AFTER spending some days in pleasant sight-seeing in London, I was to start on the 9th of November for Liverpool, to catch the steamer "Oregon," which was to leave for New York the next day; but, to my surprise, I was informed, on arrival in London, that this steamer was taken off the line, owing to some defect in her machinery, and hence my detention for a week more in London. I wish I had known of this a few days before, as some of my good-natured friends had asked me, a week ago, if I could join the Lord Mayor's Banquet, which I had to refuse with great regret.

as I knew I could not easily do it, for I had to start the same evening for Liverpool; but I had the pleasure of witnessing the Lord Mayor's Show, through the courtesy of my valued friend, Mr. John M. Cook, who very kindly asked me to come to his office, where I could have a perfect view of the procession. Again, afterwards, he very kindly entertained us to a sumptuous luncheon, which we thoroughly enjoyed. It was here I had the pleasure of being introduced to Mr. R. Saunders, the Resident of Hyderabad, and his brother, the Judge of the Chief Court of Punjaub, and his good wife.

Owing to my detention in London, I had the opportunity of visiting some more interesting places, notably Windsor Castle and Virginia Water. I was quite delighted at the drive we had in Windsor Park, which extends three miles in one straight line, through thick and huge trees and greenwood. From the Tower of the Castle you can plainly see the Statue of George the Fourth, late uncle of Her Majesty the Queen, which is erected at the end of the park. We left the cab at this point, and walked on the banks of Virginia Water, a charming little lake. On the sides of this lake you find fishing-boxes, etc., belonging to Royalty. I found a number of deer roaming in this park; in fact, they were quite tame, as they did not feel the least frightened at our approach as near as five yards distant from them.

I remained a day at the Wheatsheaf Hotel, on the Virginia Water, and spent one evening at the White Hart Hotel at Windsor, and started the next day for Hampton Court Palace. This charming little place owes its grandeur to the Palace and Park of the same name.

The most interesting things at Hampton Court are the palace and the garden attached to it, as also Bushey Park. I was informed at the palace that a number of ladies lived there (and some of the names were quite familiar to me), who had obtained their suites of apartments from Her Majesty the Queen. Princess Fredericka of Hanover was living there with her husband. I was greatly pleased with the clock dial, which is quite a novelty in its structure; and the picture gallery, which contains some of the rarest paintings that the world can produce. After spending nearly the whole of the day in visiting the Palace Gardens and Bushey Park, I went to see the little town of Hampton, situated on the bank of the Thames. I was quite delighted to see some of the residences belonging to Mr. Graves, Kyrle Bellew, the actor, and one belonging to a broker on the Stock Exchange. I was greatly pleased with what I had seen at Hampton Court. I stayed a day at the Castle Hotel and returned to London the next day.

As my time to leave Europe was drawing nigh, I had not much leisure for visiting the famous town of Oxford. I was induced especially to go and visit this place by my friends Professor and Mrs. Monier Williams. I had the pleasure of making their acquaintance in Lucerne, where they were staying at the same hotel as I did.

On arrival at Oxford I first went to the house of Professor Williams, where I was received with every kindness and courtesy by this noble lady and gentleman. After having spent some time in conversing about my travels, they asked me particularly to visit some of the colleges and other principal buildings of Oxford, which I did—viz., Christchurch, Balliol, New, and Magdalen Colleges. I was indeed greatly pleased with the interior arrangements of each of the buildings. Every college had its chapel, library, and dining-rooms. Perhaps it will not be amiss for me to say here that there are, in all, twenty-six colleges in Oxford, and about four thousand young gentlemen, the future great men of England, were taking their tuition in these colleges. Professor Williams very kindly took me over the theatre and the museum of Oxford, which were very interesting indeed. I had the pleasure of meeting at Oxford two Indian gentlemen, whose names are well known in India; and these are Messrs. M. P. Khoraghaut, a Parsee gentleman, who has successfully passed the competitive examination for the Civil Service; and the other a Hindu Pundit, Shamji Krishnanarina, Sanscrit Professor in Balliol College, now studying for the Bar.

Professor and Mrs. Williams pressed me to stay overnight at Oxford, and to dine with them the same evening, which I had to refuse with very great regret, as I had no time left on my hands to accept their hospitality; and I started the same night for Portsmouth, which place I reached late at night.

The next morning I visited the famous dockyard, a sight I never saw before. The inspector of the dockyard gave me a man, who seemed to know every inch of the yard so well that he gave me all the possible information regarding every place, ship, steamer, or man-of-war, that was in dock or in course of construction. I was quite surprised when I learnt that there were between nine to ten thousand men employed daily at the dockyard, of which one thousand four hundred were prisoners. Walking over some of the docks, I saw three large steamers (men-of-war) that were getting ready, viz., "Camperdown," ten thousand tons; "Calliope," five thousand tons; "Imperieuse," eight thousand tons; all steel plated. I had also the pleasure of seeing some of the war vessels whose names I have so often read in papers, and principally the "Minotaur," "Sultan," "Devastation," "Edinburgh," "Bacchante," in the last of which the two royal princes had their tour round the world; Her Majesty's yachts "Victoria and Albert" and "Osborne," the engineering training ship "Marlborough," and many other war ships. The arrangement in the dockyard was so nice and complete that a man could have an idea how so formidable an establishment like this worked so harmoniously, and could judge of the system which is so characteristic of the English Government. From the admiral to the inspector of the dockyard, each, and all, had to live in the same yard where the dockyard was. I here had the pleasure of seeing Captain Fisher of the "Inflexible."

After spending nearly a whole day at the dockyard, I went up the harbour and visited the two training ships, "Victory," and "Excellent," two gigantic big hulks. The inner arrangements were so perfect and orderly that it is impossible for me to say anything here, except to suggest that every traveller should try and visit one of these ships and satisfy himself. I was simply charmed at the way the English Government have their own vessels kept in such trim, and the men under such excellent discipline.

After going round the town, and over the Victoria Park, which is very nicely arranged, near the railway station, I took steamer the next morning for the Isle of Wight. After having steamed for thirty minutes, I was landed at Ryde Pier, where a train was ready to take me to Ventnor. Arriving there, I took a cab and drove round the town, and started for Bonchurch, where I stayed for a day in the hotel bearing the same name. The climate of the Isle of Wight was genial and bracing, and I was quite charmed with the scenery I saw there, and I felt sorry at not having more time to spend in this lovely island. I returned to Gosport, and from there to Portsmouth and Southsea.

The next day I left for London. Now, I had only two days, and was fully occupied in bidding good-bye to my dear friends, whose friendship I had cultivated in my short sojourn in Europe.

After completing this painful duty, I started on the morning of the 16th November for Liverpool, which place I reached the same evening, and in a few hours I started for

Manchester, to bid good-bye to two of my friends there, and whom I had faithfully promised to meet before I left Europe. The next morning, *i.e.*, the 17th, I returned to Liverpool, and after breakfasting with a few friends at the Grand Hotel, I bade farewell to dear old England.

AMERICAN TOUR.

ON the 17*th November*, 1883, I embarked on board the magnificent steamer "Servia," belonging to the Cunard Line, for the United States.

The "Servia" is of eight thousand tons and ten thousand horse power, fitted up with electric light, etc., in short, I never saw so magnificent a vessel as this. We had three hundred and eighty-nine state-room passengers, four hundred intermediate, and nearly five hundred steerage passengers. We had a splendid dining saloon, to accommodate five hundred passengers at one time, also drawing and music rooms, library and smoking saloon ; our state rooms were fitted up with electric lights, sofas, cheval glass, and all modern comforts imaginable. In short, I considered that I was not in an ordinary mail steamer, but in a fine floating palace. I should not omit to say that the food we received on board was very good, and served in excellent style.

As the steamer weighed her anchor, and slowly steamed out of the Mersey, I could not express here what feeling was ringing in my heart at that hour, but one consolation I had, that if God spared me, I hoped to see this far-famed land once more, and with extreme regret I left the English shores at about twelve noon, on the 17th November, 1883, arriving the next day at Queenstown to pick up Her Majesty's mails for America. We stopped in Queenstown for six and a half hours, and after receiving about four hundred and fifty sacks of mail packets we steamed at full speed for New York. After encountering rough passage for two days, the sea began to be calmer. On the third day, at about ten a.m., to our surprise and regret, we found a steamer with distress signals hoisted on the mast; on seeing this, our good old Captain Cook ordered the engines to be reversed, and our steamer went near her, and on enquiry, found this steamer badly wanted a surgeon to see a patient who had his skull broken from an accident met in the heavy gale. A boat was lowered immediately, and five men with the surgeon pushed off in the boat for the steamer, and after rendering all the assistance that our ship could, we steamed at full speed once more towards the banks of Newfoundland. The next day we had a very mournful task to perform, and that was to attend the funeral of a male child that died the evening previous. The ceremony was very imposing, and one I never witnessed before. At the same time, there was a birth on board the steamer, and the little guest was doing well when last reported.

We had very agreeable company on board the "Servia," every day and night. We had some sort of games in the daytime, and concerts at night, and we thus spent eight days right merrily, and safely anchored in the Bay of New York on the evening of the 26*th November*, 1883. I cannot leave the steamer without thanking the captain and the officers for the kindness and courtesy shown to me, and my special thanks are due to Mr. Keppie, the passenger agent of the company, and Mr. Field, the purser, for making my passage so comfortable. I should also mention here one fact which proved to me disagreeable, and rather prejudicial to the interests of the company; and that is, the great gambling that was going on on board the vessel when on the high seas. I am sure the captain will forbid such games.

I did not land in New York the evening the steamer anchored, as it was a wet evening; and again, it was rather late, and we all remained on board till she was safely berthed in dock the next morning. The hurry and bustle of passengers at this moment was something great. Every passenger on board had his friend or relation to receive him, and every moment to them was an hour. As they all wanted to meet with as little delay as possible, I and my friend, Mr. Roberts, who was travelling with me from Liverpool, got our luggage ready to go through the rigid examination of the custom's officers, and the necessary search being made, we were allowed to deliver the same to the expressman for conveyance to our hotel.

The day before I landed in New York was considered one of the greatest national holidays of America, being the centenarian day of the evacuation of the British forces from America, and the day was kept up in grand style. Troops of volunteers and regulars mustered very strongly, and marched through the streets with bands, colours—in fact, there was a grand procession formed for the great event, and the whole city was decorated with bunting and evergreens to give a signal proof of the event.

Immediately after my arrival in the first town of the "free land of liberty," as the Yankees style their country, I did not lose any time in visiting those gentlemen for whom I had letters of introduction, which occupied nearly two days. I met each and all, and received a warm reception; and I must thank very much my kind friends, Messrs. Dossabhoy Merwanjee and Co., Bombay, through whose medium I had the pleasure of being introduced to so many of the American firms and noblemen. Notably among them was General and his son Colonel Grant, who received me very kindly. The general was kind enough to ask me over to his house, where he introduced me to his good wife, daughter, and cousin. I finished my visits to all these gentlemen, and then commenced sight-seeing in New York.

The first interesting object I perceived was the harbour of New York. I can safely call it the most picturesque in the world. There are many imposing fortifications to this harbour, and when the weather is clear, the panoramic view of the city is unfolded; on the right you find the world-renowned and most gigantic piece of work, the Brooklyn Bridge, and on the left the Jersey city. On entering the town, the traveller's first attention is attracted to the Battery, which is a park situated on the southern extremity of the city looking out upon the bay, adorned with fine trees and verdant lawns, and protected by a granite sea wall. Passing through this pleasant park, we come to Broadway, one of the great thoroughfares of New York. A large number of extensive warehouses and offices are situated on both sides of this street. Going further, we see the beautiful Trinity Church, with its spire, about three hundred feet high. It has rich stained glass windows, and a fine chime of bells. Directly opposite this church begins Wall Street, and on the corner of this and Nassau Street is the United States Treasury, a stately white marble building in the Doric style. In the same street are the Drexel Buildings (the great bankers), the Stock Exchange, a place worth visiting, and the Custom House.

Coming back to Broadway, and going up the

Astor House, and at the end of the City Hall Park, is the new Post Office, an imposing granite building, four storeys high, and fireproof, costing seven million dollars; the upper floors are used for the United States Courts. Next to this structure is the City Hall, of three storeys, with front and ends of white marble. It has a four-dial clock, illuminated at night by electric light. This building cost five hundred thousand dollars, and is occupied by the Mayor, Common Council, and other public offices. It was here I was shown into a room on the second storey, the table on which Washington wrote his first message to Congress, the chairs used by the first Congress, and the chair in which Washington was inaugurated the first President of the United States. I also saw a fine portrait of Christopher Columbus, the discoverer of America.

Next to the City Hall, is the new Court House. Strange to say, that this grand structure was commenced in 1861, and up to this date not completed, although it has been occupied for the last seventeen years or so. It is entirely built of white marble, and the beams, staircases, etc., are of solid iron; in fact, it is a fireproof structure, costing to the State a fraudulent sum of twelve million dollars, and the contractors, or builders had to go to jail, and the case is commonly known as the "Ring Frauds," and has attracted much attention in the world. On the same road are the splendid hotels, Metropolitan and Grand

Central, Cooper Institute, and Grace Church, and at the end of the street we enter into the Union Square, with a pretty little park filled with trees, shrubbery, and green lawns. In the same park we find the bronze statues of Washington, Lincoln, and Lafayette. The square is surrounded by splendid hotels and shops, notably that of the jewellery store of Messrs. Tiffany and Co., and when this square is lit at night by gas jets, looks extremely pretty, a sight worth seeing, and gives a beautiful aspect of the square. A little further to the Union Square is another park, called Maddison Square Park. Overlooking this square is the white marble edifice of Fifth Avenue Hotel ; a little further to this, is the splendid building called the Masonic Temple, also of granite, five storeys high, rising to one hundred and fifty-five feet from the pavement. It contains splendid rooms, elegantly furnished. I was greatly attracted by the Grand Lodge Hall, which I was told measured ninety feet by eighty-four feet by thirty feet, and could accommodate about twelve hundred persons. I was here introduced to the Worshipful Master of the Lodge, Coplestown, and was quite pleased with all that I saw there. Two blocks further than this structure, is the Grand Opera House, one of the handsomest buildings I saw in that town, the interior decorations being very rich indeed.

The other street, or I should say, the fashionable

promenade of the people and resort of the higher classes, is the Fifth Avenue, beginning at Washington Square. It was here I saw the mansions belonging to Mr. Vanderbilt, the millionaire, Mrs. Stewart, Mr. Gould, and some other magnates. These structures are really fine, and no amount, or labour, is spared to make these fashionable abodes of America.

Passing through the Fifth Avenue, we come to the Central Park, one of the largest parks to be met with. I should not call it a park, but a farm or field. It is reached by two ways, either by elevated railroad or by horse cars. I preferred going there by the former, and got in one of the trains at Bleeker Street and Broadway, and alighted at the One Hundred and Fifty-fifth Street, just in the centre of the park.

After going through this gigantic field, I took an excursion on the High Bridge. This magnificent structure by which the Croton Aqueduct is carried through the Harlem River, is of granite throughout. It is one thousand four hundred and fifty feet long, and one hundred and ten feet high, supported by fourteen massive piers. At the south end is the reservoir. From this point a comprehensive view of the city may be had.

In New York I was greatly interested and surprised with two gigantic pieces of engineering works, and they are—the elevated railroad, built on iron piles on the top of the thoroughfares, passing between houses ; and the other piece of human skill and ingenuity I admired was the East River Bridge, commonly known as the "Brooklyn Bridge." Its massive towers and ponderous cables are conspicuous objects on entering the New York Harbour ; the towers are two hundred and sixty-eight feet high, and the distance across the river, between these towers, is sixteen hundred feet, and the width is eighty-five feet, affording space for two railroads, four waggon ways, and two passenger foot-paths. The height of the bridge, from high water mark to the floor of the bridge, in the centre, is one hundred and thirty-five feet. The work was commenced in the year 1871 by Mr. J. A. Roebling, a Government engineer, who was afterwards killed by an accident on the same bridge, but the gigantic work was completed by his son in May last (1883), at a cost of fourteen million dollars, which equals thirty-five million rupees. The railway is worked on the bridge across the river by means of wire ropes.

After spending nearly half a day in inspecting this splendid bridge, I went and saw the Greenwood Cemetery. I was told that this cemetery is considered the most beautiful in the world ; but, for my part, I did not find it any way better or equal to the one I saw at Genoa.

I spent a week in New York, and was quite

satisfied with the people I had met and the sights and scenes I had seen there. I did not fail to visit the best restaurant in New York—the swellish one in America is Delmonico's. I also visited the Hoffman House, Bowery Hay-market, Casino, and many other haunts of good and bad men. To have a thorough idea of the people, I also visited the best Christy Minstrels of America, called the "San Francisco Minstrels," and the Madison Theatre. I should not omit to mention about my Hotel Windsor, which is a real palatial building, luxuriantly fitted up. The dinner service was splendid. In fact, I never saw a better hotel in any other part of the globe.

After completing the sight-seeing in New York, I left, as arranged by my friends, for Boston, by the New York, Newhaven and Hartford Railroad. The scenery between these two cities is really charming. It was here I saw and had the first experience of American railroad travelling. I must mention that in America there are no different classes of railway carriages as we find in Europe and in India, but all people travel in one description of car provided by the Company; but those who wish to travel more comfortably have to buy seats for the Pullman cars, with which the railway company has no connection whatever, so practically there is a distinction between ordinary and the Pullman cars. As suggested, I always travelled in the Pullman drawing-room cars in the day-time, and in sleeping cars at night. In America, these cars are really comfortable, and add to the enjoyment of the travellers greatly. Not only this, but to express trains Pullman palace hotel cars are also attached, in which meals are served at all hours of the day, in first-rate style, and at moderate charges. The carriages are fitted up with cooking-stoves, dining-tables, chairs, etc., in a manner similar to a nice little hotel. To every seat at the table an electric call bell is fitted, to ring for the waiter or conductor. In fact, I consider railway and steamer travelling in America is more comfortable, less fatiguing, and more enjoyable than in any country in the world. After travelling in one of these cars by the express train for nearly seven hours, we arrived at Boston, the chief city of the State of Massachusetts. On the way, I met an English gentleman, Mr. Callicot, brother-in-law of Colonel Hunter, of the Punjaub force, who gave me some very valuable information about New York, Boston, and other adjoining towns; he was also going to Boston, but on a very sad mission, viz., to bury a brother, who was killed by a fall from a staircase in one of the hotels in Boston. I saw on this line how railway trains, together with the engine, are ferried across the river—a sight I never witnessed before, either in Europe or in India. The whole train, comprising nine long carriages, double the size of an ordinary

Indian railway carriage, one brake-van, and one engine, were taken on one boat, and ferried across the river in less than twenty minutes. The same engine and cars proceeded on our journey to Boston.

Boston is situated at the extremity of the Massachusetts Bay, and connected with Charlestown by a bridge (Charles River) one thousand five hundred and three feet long.

The principal thoroughfare of Boston is Washington Street, where the business houses are located. The best street in Boston is the Commonwealth Avenue, running through the newer portion of the city, and is nearly two hundred and fifty feet wide. In the middle of the street is the Park, with rows of trees. A little further from this is the Common, a park of about fifty acres, situated in the heart of the city, laid out in sloping lawns and winding walks, and shaded by magnificent trees. On Flagstaff Hill, overlooking the pond, is the Soldiers' Monument, ninety feet high, with four statues. On this very common a Public Park is laid out, with lawns and shaded trees. After visiting the State House, Boston Athenæum, containing a library of one hundred and ten thousand volumes, a reading room and City Hall, I started to see the Bunker Hill Monument, at Charlestown. It is a plain, but massive, obelisk of granite, thirty-six feet square at the base, and two hundred and twenty-one feet high. A magnificent view is obtained from the Observatory, reached by a spiral staircase of two hundred and ninety-five steps.

I returned to Boston the same evening, and drove towards the harbour, and left the same night by the Fall River line for New York. I had the good fortune to meet the steamer "Pilgrim," which is considered the most elegantly built boat in the world, and to me she appeared to be the best I have ever seen. After steaming for nearly twelve hours in the Long Island Sound and East River, we reached New York in the morning.

I started the same evening for Washington, as I was anxious to see the working of the Congress, the election of the Speaker, and other members of the Senate. General Grant had also very kindly given me a letter of introduction to the officers of the Senate, and also asked me not to fail to see this grand sight of America, and so I hastened my journey thither, as the Congress was to assemble and the election was to be carried on the next morning. After spending the night in the sleeping car, I arrived the next morning at Washington, the capital of the United States. After a good breakfast at Ebbitt House, I started towards the Capitol, one of the magnificent public edifices in America. On entering the Hall, I presented my card with the letter of General Grant, and Mr. Hooker, the Sergeant-at-Arms, very kindly received me, and offered a seat in the lobby, from which I could see and hear everything. The hall was crowded, and many ladies and gentlemen had to wait outside for want of space. Immediately after twelve o'clock the roll was called to see if all the members of the Congress were present. This occupied nearly an hour; then the election of the Speaker of the House took place, which occupied nearly another hour. After the election of the Speaker and other officers, the taking of the oath by the newly-elected members commenced; and soon after that, a speech from the newly-elected Speaker and working of the House followed. In this way, nearly the whole of the day was spent; but I must say that all I saw was quite interesting and new to me. I was introduced to General Warner, of Ohio, and many other magnates of greater or lesser degree. After this I went over this gigantic edifice of marble. It consists of a main building and two wings, measuring seven hundred and fifty feet long; on the steps of the central portico are groups of statuary. Another object of attraction in this building was the bronze door, which forms an entrance to the Rotunda. It is nearly eighteen feet long, and weighs twenty thousand pounds, costing thirty thousand dollars. In this building are the offices of several officers of the State, the Senate Room, a library, and many other chambers, all elegantly furnished. The total cost of this Capitol was thirteen million dollars, equal to thirty-three million rupees, and took nearly thirty years to complete the works.

After having tendered my thanks to the officers of the Senate, I left the building, and went over to the United States Treasury, a magnificent building, built of white marble, with two storeys. It has nearly two hundred rooms, and the first is the cash room, lined throughout with marble. The gold room was another sight to be witnessed, where some millions of dollars in gold were to be seen. Another room was the bond room, which was shown to me by a special permit of the Governor. The next interesting thing I noticed was the printing of the United States Currency Notes. It was wonderful indeed; and again the process of destroying old notes, which was also done by means of machinery. I was equally surprised when I was informed that nearly eleven hundred men and seven hundred girls were employed at this Treasury to do the current work. After thanking the Governor, who so kindly allowed me to be shown round this interesting place, I went to the Executive Mansion of the President of the United States, commonly known as the "White House." It is a huge square block of white building of two storeys; the grounds are beautifully laid out, and contain fountains and an extensive conservatory. The blue, green, and red rooms are on the same floor, and are splendidly furnished. Westward of the White House is the War Office, a splendid building of massive granite, of four storeys, nearly six hundred feet long, and three hundred and fifty feet high. In this building are the offices of the Secretary of State, the Ambassadors, and the offices of the Army and Navy. The next place I visited was the Patent Office; the Model room, which is nearly one thousand four hundred feet long, divided into four large halls, fitted up with cases containing innumerable numbers of models, representing every department of mechanical art. My attention was drawn in one of the rooms to the printing press belonging to Benjamin Franklin, and the military uniform worn by Washington on resigning his commission as Commander-in-Chief.

I left the place quite pleased, and saw the Post Office, another imposing edifice of white marble; and the Washington Monument, which, when completed, will be the loftiest in the world; but nobody seems to know when it will be finished, as the authorities are quite short of funds. I drove through the town, along the Pennsylvania Avenue, which is the busiest and most fashionable street in the city; handsome shops, theatres, and other buildings, are situated in this street.

After spending nearly two days in this city, I left for Baltimore, the chief city of Maryland, *viâ* Baltimore and Ohio Railroad. Here I met Mr. Alex. Godby and Mr. Spence, who were very kind in offering to render any assistance I might want. I was introduced to them by my friend Mr. Ffinch.

Baltimore is really a nice little town, full of business. I drove through the town, and the cleanliness and the people I saw reminded me of Rotterdam and the Hague in Europe. In Baltimore I visited the Washington Monument, which is three hundred and twenty feet high, built entirely of brick, with outward casing of marble, costing two hundred thousand dollars, the battle monument erected in memory of those who fell in defending the city from the British in 1814. Facing the Washington Memorial is the magnificent marble building of the Peabody Institute, founded and endowed by George Peabody, the great philanthropist. It contains a free library of nearly sixty thousand volumes, a lecture hall and music room. The City Hall is another fine building of which Baltimore can boast, built entirely of marble, of four storeys. A magnificent view can be had of the city from the balcony of this building. After lunching at the Merchants' Club with Mr. Godby, I started for Philadelphia, *via* Pennsylvania Railroad, arriving there after a run of two and a half hours.

Philadelphia, the largest city of the United States, lies on the west bank of the river Delaware. It is a thorough business place, and the bustle of men, carts, cars, and all vehicles, can be observed at all hours of the day. The fashionable promenade of this city is the Chestnut Street, where splendid hotels and retail shops are to be seen.

On coming out of the railway station I was quite surprised and amazed at the huge marble edifice called the New City Hall. On enquiry I was told that it had cost ten million dollars. It is a solid square marble block of four storeys, and covers nearly five acres of land. The length of the building is four hundred and ninety feet, width four hundred and seventy feet; the central tower is four hundred and fifty feet high. I never saw such a gigantic marble building as this before. Close to this is the shop of John Wanamaker, the great dry goods merchant. I was surprised, on entering his monstrous shop, when I was informed by one of the lady assistants, that nearly eleven hundred hands are employed. What must be the trade there, and what quantity of goods sold daily? really I have no idea whatever.

I then visited the Fairmount Park, which is said to be the largest park in the world, covering nearly three thousand acres of land. There are a good many statues, lawns, flower beds, and zoological gardens, all artistically and tastefully laid out, and really a charming resort for a tired and weary soul. After dining at Girard House, I left the same night for New York, at which place I arrived at midnight. I spent a day in New York, and started the next day for a tour in Canada.

CANADA.

The first city I visited was Montreal, the largest city and commercial metropolis of British North America. The principal building I witnessed here was the Court House in Notre Dame Street, a beautiful large building, built at the cost of three million dollars. A little further to this is the City Hall. The Roman Catholic Cathedral of Notre Dame is another large and magnificent edifice, seating twelve thousand persons. It has six towers, and in one of them is a fine chime of bells, the largest of which weighs thirty thousand pounds.

After this I went to the Mount Royal, through the cemetery, and had a picturesque birds-eye view of the town of Montreal. The Mount Royal stands seven hundred and fifty feet high. The most interesting object and piece of human skill I saw here was the Victoria Bridge. I can safely call it the eighth wonder of the world. It is built on the river St. Lawrence. On enquiry I was informed that it measured nine thousand two hundred feet, or nearly two miles. It rests on twenty-three piers, the centre span being three hundred and thirty feet in length. The cost of the bridge was sixty-three million dollars. It was opened by the Prince of Wales in 1860.

After this, I visited the Lachme Rapids, which are the most turbulent and dangerous in the river. I quite forgot to mention above, that no sooner had my train glided into the railway shed at Montreal, I noticed snow lying on the railway track about two to three feet, and was rather surprised, when getting out of the train and going to the hotel, to see vehicles which had no wheels, and these are commonly known as sleighs. This was the first time in my life that I had seen them, and found them so comfortable and warm, that I drove in one all day. The scenery on Mount Royal was something charming: the milky snow spread on the hills and on the roofs of the houses, the sun shining on them with all his mighty lustre, and affording such a pleasing sight that I never can forget; and, to crown all, I saw lovely Canadian ladies, in their holiday garb, slowly skating on the rinks; some riding on the mountain and some following on foot. All this was to me a dream, for the next day I did not see anything like it, and perhaps I shall never see such a sight. I was really pleased with all I saw in this snowy region.

The next day I started for Ottawa, by the Grand Trunk Railway, at which place I arrived after a run of four hours. This neat little town is situated on the River Ottawa, at the mouth of the Rideau. The principal streets of the town are the Sparks and Sussex. The former is a fashionable promenade, and has many leading shops. It is a great centre of the lumber trade, and has many saw-mills and manufactories of iron castings. The one I had the pleasure of visiting belonged to Mr. Eddy, and it was fitted throughout with the electric light.

The chief feature of the city is the Parliament House and the buildings adjoining to it, costing four million dollars. One of the attractions in the building is the Library, a handsome structure, containing forty thousand volumes. A little further than this is the Rideau Hall, the official residence of the Governor-General, and which is reached after crossing the river Rideau.

The Cathedral of Notre Dame is another handsome edifice in the city, with double spires of two hundred feet high. The interior of it is very imposing.

The scenery in the vicinity of Ottawa is picturesque and grand; and once more I got a sleigh, drawn by a pair of smart horses, and drove up to the Chaudière Falls, over the height of forty feet, and two hundred feet in width. Below the falls is a suspension bridge, from which a grand view is obtained. After driving through the city, I returned to my hotel (Russel House), and spent the evening with an English officer who served for many years in India (Captain Watson, Fifty-eighth Regiment), and started the next morning for Toronto, the capital of the Province of Ontario, and situated on a circular bay on the north-west of Lake Ontario. King, Young, Front, and Queen streets are the principal ones in the city. The finest building in this city, or in Canada, is the University of Toronto, standing in a large and beautiful park, and approached by College Avenue, lined with a double row of trees. The University contains a library of twenty thousand volumes.

Adjoining the University grounds is the Queen's Park, tastefully laid out and splendidly shaded. In the middle of the park stands a beautiful statue of Britannia, erected in memory of the Canadians who fell in repelling the Fenians in 1866.

The other handsome edifice in this town is the St. James Cathedral, with a lofty tower and spire, surrounded by shady grounds. A little westward to the city is the Lunatic Asylum, a large, handsome building, with several hundred acres of ornamental grounds. After driving through the town, and seeing many other fine buildings, as the Post Office (Toronto Street), City Hall (Front Street), and the Custom House, I left in the evening for Hamilton, which neat little town I reached the same night, and, after spending the night there, I left for Niagara Falls, a household word in America, and a name known in almost every quarter of the globe. I stayed at the Prospect House, on the Canadian side, from which place I commanded an excellent view of the Horse Shoe Fall.

Next morning I prepared myself to go underneath these falls; and to accomplish this risky job, I engaged the services of two stalwart English guides. After putting on the india-rubber clothing, which was supplied by the men, I went underneath, and the appearance was simply wonderful. I was informed by the guides that the descent of the cataract was one hundred and fifty-eight feet, and two thousand feet wide, and it is stated that fifteen hundred million cubic feet of water pass over the ledges every hour. The sight of these falls is really grand and picturesque to behold. After completing this hazardous task, I went over to Goat Island, which is reached by means of an iron bridge, which in itself was an object of great interest. From this bridge a splendid view is to be seen of the rapids, which I consider a most impressive feature of the Niagara scenery. I returned to the Canadian side by the new suspension bridge. It is a marvel of architecture, nearly fifteen hundred feet long, and two hundred feet above the river. A magnificent view of the falls and of the gorge is obtained by ascending one of the towers of the bridge, which is one hundred and five feet high. Below the falls are to be seen the Whirlpool Rapids; by descending the elevator, which leads from the top to the base of the cliff, a closer view is obtained of these wonderful rapids. I was shown the exact spot where poor Captain Webb took his last plunge, out of which he never succeeded to rise. From the rapids, I drove up to the Burning Springs, which were three miles away from this spot, and it is reached by River Road. These famous burning springs, whose waters emit into the air sulphuretted hydrogen gas, which burns with a brilliant flame. The spring is very nicely arranged to show off the phenomenon, and its true colour and light; and I was greatly pleased, and felt interested in the different ways it was shown to me. On tasting this spring water, I found as if it was mixed with sulphur.

I must not omit to say that great extortion is practised in this part by the guides, as well as the people who are in charge of the falls, rapids, and springs. Again, the cab hire is very high; and it is desirable to make explicit agreement before starting to see any of the wonders of America on this side, and it is advisable for those who can spare more time to walk and see all these sights, which are within the compass of an easy walk; and thus a great deal of annoyance and imposition is avoided. I spent nearly two days at this place.

I left the next morning for Chicago by the Great Western division of the Grand Trunk Railroad of Canada. Some charming scenery is perceived on the way to Chicago by this line. I found another most interesting thing on this line, and which was, that the railroad between Windsor and Detroit, a distance of one hundred and ten miles, was in one straight line without a single curve or bend. At Detroit, the whole of the train is ferried over in a boat, and the route is resumed on the line of the Michigan Central Railroad. After passing through Cleveland and Toledo, we arrived at Chicago early next morning, and put up at the Palmer House, an immense fireproof structure, occupying entirely the whole block in State Street. The building is one of the most imposing in the city, and its interior decorations are very grand. Chicago, the principal city of Illinois, is the greatest railway centre on the Continent of America. It is pleasantly situated on the shores of Lake Michigan, at the mouth of the river Chicago. Commercial houses and fashionable retail shops are all situated in State Street. The other important streets of the city are the Lake, Clarke, Randolph, Bearborn, Madison, and Washington. The principal attractive buildings of the city are the City Hall, the United States Custom House and Post Office, costing five million dollars; the Chamber of Commerce, its interior decorations are very elaborate. The great hall, in which the Board of Trade meets, is one hundred and forty-two feet by eighty-seven by forty-five feet. The ceiling is beautifully painted, representing the trade of the city and the great fire of Chicago. The Exposition Building is a fine structure, built entirely of iron and glass. It is eight hundred feet by two hundred feet, and surmounted by a dome of one hundred and sixty feet in height. Chicago can boast of many fine churches, but Trinity Church is extremely pretty, and has a noble interior. The Public Library and Chicago University are two other grand buildings of the city. The former contains ninety-two thousand volumes, including many German, English, French, and Bohemian books. The latter occupies a beautiful site near Lake Michigan; the main building was completed in 1866, at a cost of one hundred thousand dollars. The United States Marine Hospital, a little beyond Lincoln Park, is another of the largest and costliest structures in the country; it is nearly three hundred and fifty feet long, and cost about three hundred and seventy-two thousand dollars.

There are three splendid parks in Chicago, viz., the Lincoln, Union, and Jefferson, but the best is the Lincoln Park, on the lake shore, occupying nearly three hundred acres of land, and has splendid drives, walks, fine trees, artificial hills and mounds, miniature lakes, summer houses, and shady rambles.

After going through these parks, I drove to the

water works of Chicago, which is considered one of the largest features in America, and one of the wonders of the world. They comprise a stone water tower one hundred and sixty feet high, up which the water is forced by powerful engines, having pumping capacity of seventy-five million gallons daily, and flows thence through the pipes to every part of the city. A splendid view of the city lake is to be had from the top of the tower.

I was particularly asked not to leave Chicago without paying a visit to the Stock Union Yard, which is considered one of the best and most interesting sights of America, and in obedience to these instructions, I drove to this world-known place. I here met the manager of Messrs. Armour and Co., who very kindly asked one of their assistants to show me each and all the interesting sights of the yard. At first we entered into the live-stock yard, which comprised six hundred acres of land. They have a capacity for twenty-five thousand cattle, one hundred thousand hogs, twenty-two thousand sheep, and twelve hundred horses, in these yards. I found a hotel, banks, and a board of trade, also a post and telegraph office; in fact, it was a little town. The other most interesting sight, yet cruel to behold, was the slaughtering and dressing of cattle, and the pork packing. The hogs are driven up an inclined plane to a pen in the upper part of the packing house, a chain attached to the pulley in a sliding frame near the ceiling, is slipped over one leg, and the poor hog is jerked up, his throat cut, the body lowered into a large vat of boiling water, lifted out, scraped, dressed, and hung up to cool. After going through this process, it is cut to pieces, salted, and packed, and in this way, some thousands are shipped to different parts of the world. I was informed that nearly nine hundred cattle and seven thousand hogs were killed daily in the stock-yard of Messrs. Armour and Co., and to carry this out, and work the business, they have to employ four thousand five hundred hands. When leaving this yard, I took a glance at the stores, and I saw some thousand cases of meat, some hundreds of barrels of lard, sausages, etc., ready to be despatched to any part of the world at a moment's notice. Truck loads of ice were to be seen there to carry meat to different parts of the Continent. The other sight I saw in Chicago was the grain elevator. I here had an idea in what way the immense grain trade is carried on. There are about twenty buildings, all situated on the bank of the Chicago River, connected with the side trucks of the railway, where the grain is unloaded and shipped in steamers.

After going through all these interesting sights I returned to my hotel, and left at midnight for Denver by Chicago, Burlington, and Quincy Railroad. To our train Pullman palace sleeping and hotel cars were attached, and we passed through some picturesque scenery. I here saw and crossed the great river Mississippi at the largest city of Iowa, called Burlington. We stopped for a few hours, and resumed our journey, and after a rattling speed, in about thirty-nine hours, we arrived at Denver. I stopped here for half a day, and drove over this neat little town. After having my baggage re-checked for San Francisco, I resumed journey for Salt Lake City, *viâ* Denver and Rio Grande Railroad. (This line is built on the narrow gauge). The scenery on this line is simply indescribable, especially when our little train climbed to the top of the summit, a height of about ten thousand eight hundred and fifty-seven feet, where nothing but snow-clad mountains were perceptible, and the sparkling rays of the sun shining on them presented a brilliant scene worth visiting.

After passing through the Marshall Pass, we arrived early in the morning at Salt Lake City, the capital of Utah Territory, and the chief town of the Mormons. The principal attractions of this city are, the Tabernacle, Camp Douglas, and the great Salt Lake.

The Tabernacle is built entirely of wood, except the fifty sandstone pillars which support the immense oval-shaped dome. This huge wooden building can accommodate about fifteen thousand men. It is used for worship, lectures, and debates. The Tabernacle organ is one of the largest in America. A little further from this is the New Temple, estimated to cost ten million dollars, and of which three storeys are now up; but by the way the work is now going on, I do not think it will be complete for the next thirty years, for there were very few men working on it, as I was told they were short of funds.

In the same street were the Museum, Theatre and Opera House, and the Co-operative Store. None of them I found of great importance. After driving through the principal streets, viz., Main and Temple, I went to the Douglas Camp, about two miles distant from the city, situated on a fine hill overlooking the city, and had a grand view of the town and the lake.

From this I drove to the station and took train, *viâ* Utah Western Railroad, to Lake Point. I here found a fine hotel and bath-house. The lake is situated in mountains about four thousand two hundred feet above the level of the sea; several rivers flow into it, but it has no outlet. The water is very shallow, and in many parts not more than three feet deep. I never saw water so clear, yet so exceedingly salt. It is so buoyant that a man may float on it at full length upon his back, having his head and neck, and both arms to the elbow, entirely out of water.

I returned to the city in the evening, and went over to the house of Brigham Young, the Mormon

King, who died seven years ago, leaving behind his sixteen wives and forty-eight children to mourn their loss. Opposite this house (Beehive) is a large and handsome building, which belonged to the King's favourite wife, and known as Amelia Palace. It is now occupied by the present Governor Taylor and his four wives!

I left this city early next morning for Ogden. Here we changed cars and proceeded on our journey to San Francisco by the Central Pacific Railroad (broad gauge). After passing through the towns of Elko and Reno, we entered the golden land (mines of America) called California. When passing the Golden Run and the Dutch Flat, I saw nothing but some hundreds of gold and silver mines, worked by thousands of Chinamen under the directions of Americans. After going through Auburn, a name so familiar to those who have read, I saw some of the beauties of California passing through this charming place.

We arrived in the evening at Sacramento, the capital of California. We dined, and resumed our journey to San Francisco, *viâ* Oakland. I here saw another wonder. When reaching the Straits Carquenez, the whole of our train, consisting of thirteen long carriages, together with two engines, was ferried across by a huge river steamer, which is considered the largest ferry boat in the world. It is four hundred and fifty feet long, can accommodate forty-eight loaded waggons; the diameter of the paddle is fourteen feet, and this huge boat is worked by four engines. It is a wonderful boat in its build, size, and shape.

After a long ride of nearly sixty hours, we arrived safely, on the evening of 16th December, 1883, at San Francisco. I stayed at the Palace Hotel, which is considered one of the largest in the world. This gigantic building, I am told, can easily accommodate twelve hundred persons at one time. When I was there seven hundred people were in the hotel.

San Francisco, the chief city of California and commercial metropolis of the Pacific coast, is situated on the bay of the same name. The streets are broad and well laid out; the leading thoroughfare is the Market Street, with handsome buildings, the Treasury and Montgomery Streets. The fashionable promenade, principal banks, and insurance brokers' offices, are located in California and Pine Streets. The Palace Hotel stands at the corner of Market and Montgomery Streets. It is of nine storeys, costing three million two hundred and fifty thousand dollars. The other palatial buildings of this city are the Baldwin Hotel, costing three hundred and fifty thousand dollars; the Mercantile Library, four storeys high, containing fifty thousand volumes; the Merchants' Exchange; the Bank of California, and the United States Branch Mint.

After driving through the principal quarters of the

city, I went by cable car to Golden Gate Park, which comprises one thousand and forty-three acres beautifully laid out in walks, drives, lawns, and shady nooks. A splendid conservatory is also erected here, and a decent restaurant completes the arrangement of the park. Close to the park is the Cliff House; it is six miles from the city. A fine admirable boulevard is kept, where hundreds of vehicles and pedestrians are to be met. A restaurant attached to this house provides excellent dinners and other refreshments. About fifty yards from the house lies the Seal Rock, on which some hundreds of seals are seen basking in the sun or wriggling over the rock. A little further to this lies the Golden Gate, a beautiful entrance to San Francisco harbour.

I had the opportunity of visiting the China Town of San Francisco. It is about two miles distant from the city, where no less than forty thousand people are found. More curious to me were their theatre, gambling houses, and opium cellars. I do not think I should ever like to visit those miserable holes again. In a cellar, greasy and dirty, and filled with smoke, about a hundred of these men will be found, sitting around tables, betting. The opium cellars are fitted up with benches or shelves; on each of these will be found a couple of Chinamen lying on the boards, with a wooden box for a pillow. They smoke in pairs; while one smokes and prepares the opium, the other is dozing in a half-drunken sleep. Even in the theatre smoking of either opium or tobacco is found. The performance in these so-called theatres is simply clashing of cymbals, beating of drums, gongs, blowing of trumpets, and some other hideous kinds of noises. I was greatly disgusted on seeing this, as I was not accustomed to them.

When at San Francisco I had the opportunity of being present, by the kind invitation of Colonel Wittington, at the grand reception given to General Hancock. It was arranged on a grand scale at the Pavilion, where no less than six thousand people had met to give a hearty reception to the old veteran soldier. It was here I had the opportunity of seeing some of the American volunteers, regular soldiers, and officers of different army corps. Fortunately, I had a seat very close to the General, and I had a chance of seeing the march past of the troops, which were mustered strongly, about three thousand in number; but I was greatly disappointed, on seeing some of the volunteers and their officers, at the deplorable ignorance of military tactics. I can safely say that our Sind volunteer corps, though quite young, could better show off in discipline and military tactics than the Americans can, with all the lot of gold lace and other beauties on their persons. The meeting dispersed late at night, after a good speech from the General, thanking the people for their hearty reception;

and the event ended in a sumptuous supper, provided at the Palace Hotel, where the General was staying.

After spending six days in San Francisco, I commenced to prepare for a long sea voyage to Japan, and for this I had to arrange with the O. and O. Steamship Company to provide me with a berth in one of their fast steamers leaving for Yokohama, and, to my good fortune, I found the magnificent steamer, "Oceanic," was to leave for the above port. On seeing the passenger agent, Mr. Horsburgh, who was really very kind to me in giving me one of the best state-rooms that the steamer had; he very kindly asked me to see the room before he would register it in my name, and in case I did not approve of it he would give me the one I should select or choose; and he requested his able assistant, Mr. Sylvester, to accompany me to the steamer, and show me round all that was to be seen. On boarding this vessel, this young man introduced me to almost all the officers of the steamer, and showed me all the state-rooms that were available; but I did not find any better than the one originally selected for me by Mr. Horsburgh. It was immediately next to the captain's. He again assisted me in giving much valuable information about Japan and China, and, after thanking him and Mr. Sylvester for their kindness, I now bade good-bye to San Francisco, and started on my voyage to Yokohama.

I should not omit to say a few words here about the people, manners, and customs of the Americans. For fairness sake, I must say that I received great attention and kindness at the hands of many American gentlemen, in almost all the towns. Several of them had always shown great zeal and attention for my tour, and assisted me materially in chalking out my different tours and routes, and left nothing to make my journey as pleasant and comfortable as possible; and all this I do not think I shall ever forget.

I have said before, that this land is considered as the Free Land of Liberty, but I find that there is too much liberty given or allowed to middle-class people, which I do not in the least like. For instance, a railway conductor or porter sitting and dining in the same car, at the same table, and at the same time, as the first-class passengers. Again, these men spoke to passengers in a tone as if they were the directors of the railway; for every hour these magnates come and sit alongside the passengers. This may be nothing in the eyes of those who are in the habit of mixing so freely with these men, but to me it was rather unique and unpleasant. In the same way, a doorkeeper or a barman of the hotel will shake hands and greet a colonel or a major of the army as if they were of equal rank and position.

A fellow travelling companion enquired what I thought of this country. I said it was very good and interesting, but pointed out the same defect as I have just before said. He quietly told me that he agreed with me, and I was quite right; and he felt sometimes very bad over it; but again, he said, if I were to stay longer I shall be quite used to these customs and manners. I thanked him for the suggestion, and added, the sooner I cleared out of the country the better, or else I may be led to do the same mischief in my quiet little town.

Another most novel thing I perceived in America was, that there is more military element than civil, although the so-called military officers are attired entirely in civilian clothes. At every hotel, restaurant, or business place, you are sure to meet generals, colonels, majors, and captains. I was quite astonished to see how these officers obtained their commissions. Some colonels were twenty years of age, some majors had no sign of moustache, and some colonels had to sweat day and night to watch their guests' baggage safely conveyed to different railway depôts. There is one defect, and a serious one too, I found among these men of the " Free Land of Liberty," and that is, presumption. They think there is no country in the world like theirs, or any people like their own living on the face of the earth that can prove equal to their great men or generals. I did not like this idea, and listened to all they said, but knew more, and how far I should credit them.

EASTERN TOUR.

I LEFT San Francisco on the noon of *22nd December*, 1883, with sixteen state room and about seven hundred (Chinamen) steerage passengers. The way they were quartered in the fore and after part of the steamer was sickening. They were packed like sardines in a tin box. The passenger agent of the company, who had come on board with his despatches, asked me to have a glance at these places before the steamer started, and at his suggestion, I did go; but I got sick on entering the place, for the air was so stifling, and people were jammed in their little berths so close, that any man of good strength could easily break down.

On the 23rd we had head winds all the day, which made the passage rather disagreeable; but since then it was much pleasanter, and all enjoyed the trip immensely. Our young Captain Davison, who is fond of cricketing, kept all my fellow-passengers very lively with this manly game on board the steamer, though not played to any great advantage. Our jovial purser, Mr. Ramage, and good-humoured chief engineer, Mr. Allen, and the good old soul, Mr. Thomson, the chief officer, and the young doctor of the steamer, Mr. Dudley, all tried their best to make the passage as comfortable and agreeable for passengers as possible; and for my part, I was so much pleased with them, that it was with great regret I parted, in hopes of meeting once more to enjoy their company.

Christmas and New Year's Day, which we had the good fortune to spend at sea, and in this magnificent steamer, were kept up right merrily; our dining-saloon and the sitting-room were tastefully decorated with the flags of all nationalities and evergreens, and the good old chief steward provided sumptuous dinners on these two occasions; in fact, we had a most charming passage throughout our voyage on the Pacific Ocean, and enjoyed the trip immensely. I cannot forget Christmas and New Year's Day which we had the good fortune to spend at sea, as I have said above. On the voyage we had three deaths among the steerage passengers, and in accordance with Chinese customs, and with the agreement made by the agents of the steamers, their bodies were not buried at sea as usual, but were embalmed, and packed in cases to be landed at Hong Kong. The company receives for each of these cases, or "stiffs," as the Americans call them, twelve and a half dollars, and the doctor gets the same amount for embalming the body, and the undertakers, as they are termed, six dollars for placing the dead body in the case, and lashing it up at the extreme end of the vessel. Of course, nobody loses anything by having a good many of such "stiffs" on board the steamer.

After steaming for twenty-two days on the Pacific Ocean, including the day we lost *en route* in long. 180°, lat. 32° 45', we arrived safely in Yokohama Harbour on the morning of the 14th January, 1884. When nearing the harbour, we saw the world-renowned steep mountain of Fujujama, covered with snow, and considered the highest mountain in Japan, thirteen thousand feet.

Yokohama, the first and important port of Japan, is situated on the Bay of Yeddo, and commands a picturesque view of the extensive harbour, which could easily accommodate vessels of the largest size, about one thousand to fifteen hundred in number. The day we entered this fine harbour was a Russian holiday, and all the Russian and Japanese gunboats and other war vessels, were decorated with bunting, and produced a charming appearance in the harbour. We here noticed many other war vessels, representing English, French, Turkish, and Danish nationalities. In fact, I never witnessed such a motley gathering of gunboats in any harbour before. We landed at the Custom's jetty, and having gone through the usual examination by the Custom's authorities, I proceeded to the Hotel Windsor, which is pleasantly situated on the Bund. After partaking of lunch, I drove round the town, which is divided into three parts, viz., the Bluff, Settlement, and the Native Town. The Bluff is situated on a fine hill, overlooking the sea, covered with rice fields, flowers, and fruit trees, and some splendid buildings erected by the European population. The drive through the rice fields on this hill is extremely pretty. In former times, detachments of English soldiers were quartered on the hill for the protection of their people, who were then trading; but time went along, and brought the two governments on more friendly terms, and there was no longer any necessity for those troops, and they were ordered off home. The residences on the picturesque hill are pleasantly located, surrounded by tastefully laid-out gardens. A splendid view is also to be obtained of the Settlement, Yeddo Bay, and the surrounding country from the hill; on the other side of it is the country and the United States Hospital.

The Settlement, where the offices of different consuls and merchants are located, is entirely built or laid out on the European plan, fine wide streets and walks, nicely paved, and lit with gas; the principal ones are the Bund and the Main; on the former, the leading hotels, clubs, and some handsome European residences are situated, facing the harbour, where a number of men-of-war and merchant steamers of various nations are to be seen ; the latter contains many large and fine buildings, most of which are occupied as godowns for merchants, and offices. North of this street is the Japanese Imperial Post Office and the Telegraph Office, and in front of these two is the handsome building called "Machi Keewanto" (the Town Hall), surmounted by a clock tower. I was greatly pleased to see the tea-firing godowns of Messrs. Middleton and Co., where a large quantity of tea is fired or dried over in these godowns, previous to shipment, a sight quite novel to me.

The Native Town is an object of interest. All the houses on this side are entirely built of wood and bamboo—very little of chunam, sand, or stone is known on this side—but cries and reports of conflagrations are daily heard. There are two main streets in this town, where numbers of shops containing lacquer ware, bronzes, porcelain, and other curiosities are to be seen. I was also greatly pleased at some of the shops where beautiful silks were exhibited. All this shows how and to what extent this nation is advanced in industry and skill.

After spending five days in Yokohama, I left for Yeddo, or recently known as Tokio, the capital of Japan. I here had the first experience of travelling on a Japanese railway, which I am informed is built entirely by an English company for this Government.

The line is constructed on the narrow gauge, carriages comfortable, and roads well kept. After passing through Kanazawa, Kawasahi, and a few other stations, we arrived at Tokio, a large commercial metropolis, and capital town of Japan. In the centre of the town is the Citadel, protected by moats and embankments, faced with massive stone walls. The moats are crossed by wooden bridges. The present Mikado is living in one of the palaces here, which is void of any beauty or attraction, although one is now contemplated which will be more worthy of a monarch than the present ordinary wooden-built house; as I have said above, fires are of frequent occurrence, for the houses are built entirely of light, combustible articles, and it is not uncommon that some thousands of houses become a heap of ruins before the flames can be extinguished.

The chief attraction of Tokio is the place called Shiba, and I can safely call it the garden of Tokio, as the roads here are clean, wide, and well laid out, trees planted on both sides of the road, affording a delightful abode. Pretty gardens full of flowers are seen in almost every direction, and priests, with shaved heads and long robes, are met at every turning. I was ushered to a place called the Zoogoji, the celebrated temple of Tokio, where the tombs of the Mikados and their wives are to be seen I was shown here by a priest some six graves surrounded by two hundred stone lanterns, and some of them were made of solid bronze about six feet high, and more resembled post pillars. In the temple of Zoogoji ornamental ceilings and the richly carved panels are the objects of great attraction.

From Shiba we drove to a place called Kaita Kush, where we entered a museum devoted entirely to the industrial and natural resources of Japan. The collection is large and varied, and here we can form an idea to what extent the Japanese nation is skilful and industrious. The gardens surrounding the museum are tastefully laid out, and fruits and flowers are brought to the highest state of cultivation. A few large bears are shown in the extreme end of the garden.

From the museum we went to a little hillock called the Stazo Yemma. Two flights of stone steps lead us to the top. A charming view is to be had of the bay, with its men-of-war, forts, and fishing boats. Turning to the west we saw the towers of large castles, the Engineering College, and the Russian and Italian Legations.

After having a view of this picturesque scenery, we descended the hill and drove up to Oyens. We entered this place through a large black gate, in which we noticed the marks of bullets. I was told it was here the soldiers of the Mikado had many struggles. A little further from this place is a large building and a large bronze statue of Dai Butai, about twenty-five feet high.

From Oyens we drove up to a hilly place called Asaksa. Here we saw a large temple, considered the most celebrated in Japan. The goddess here worshipped by the superstitious Japanese is an image entirely made of pure gold, and about two inches in height. Around this temple are numerous gay shops for the sale of toys, ornaments, etc. The most interesting of all was the one which contained life size wax representations similar to those exhibited in Europe and America, but differently attired; that is, the body of these figures were planted with green foliage and trimmed in such a manner that gave a beautiful aspect. Near this temple some thousands of tamed pigeons are seen flying about, as they are held sacred, and women are seen selling peas and rice in earthen pots to feed them.

The Japanese do not visit this place for pious motives only, but their main object is for pleasure, for we find different theatres, circus, acrobatic performances, tea and wine shops, and some hundred varieties of entertainments.

After visiting this famous temple, I went to the offices of the Finance, Home, and Public Works Departments. These buildings are very handsome. The other object which attracted my attention in Tokio was the tram-cars. I think the company must be doing a roaring business, for each and every car I witnessed was packed with men like herrings in a cask, and the car was dragged by a miserable Japanese pony. I dined at the Hotel Sei-yo-ken.

The next day I left for Yokohama and Yenoshima, *viâ* Kanazawa and Inamura, in a carriage, arriving at Kanazawa in about two hours. This pretty little village is situated on the shores of Goldsborough Inlet, and I visited a large temple there. From this we drove to Kawakura, which is situated in a valley enclosed by hills. The great attraction here is the Shinto Temple. The approach to it is imposing and beautiful, and the temple is reached by a flight of fifty-eight steps. A little further from this temple is the famous bronze image of Buddha, commonly known among the Japanese as Dai Butai. The height of this image is fifty feet, and weighs about thirty tons. From Kawakura we drove through Yenoshima, a beautiful little village situated on the seaside. The charming scenery we saw here repays all the trouble. This island is clothed in perpetual green foliage, and gives a beautiful aspect. We returned to Yokohama late in the evening.

After staying in this place for two days, I started for Kobi by steamer, a distance of about three hundred and forty-eight miles. This is a nice town and important port for Osaka and Kioto. After spending the day in visiting the Moon Temple and the Waterfall, I started for Osaka, the trading centre of Japan. I visited the castle, a massive building of stone. The next place I saw was the Mint, which is worked on the same principle as that of the United States. The houses are entirely built of wood, like Tokio and other towns ; and after going through the town, I left for Kobi, and started next day through the inland sea of Japan to Nagasaki. The scenery I saw in this trip of the inland sea is indescribable, and the way the steamers are dexterously handled through the numerous islands and narrow sea is really to be admired. I saw hills and mountains covered with green foliage, and in some parts I saw a good many villages. I was informed by the captain that the sea is very deep, and in some instances no depth could be fathomed. We steamed for two days through the inland sea, and safely arrived at Nagasaki, a port of Japan, most charmingly situated. It is surrounded by mountains covered with greenness. It is a coaling port, and many steamers from and to Shanghai stay for a day or two to coal and receive provisions. I stayed in Nagasaki for nearly thirty-six hours, and bade good-bye to Japan on the morning of the 29th January, 1884, and left for Shanghai by the Japanese mail steamer "Hiroshima Maree." Captain J. Wynn and other officers of this vessel were very kind and courteous, and after steaming for three days, arrived at the mouth of the river Yangtse Kiang, where we anchored for the night, and proceeded slowly the next morning up the river, and reached Shanghai the same evening. I must say a few words about the people of Japan. They are a shrewd, skilful, ingenious, honest, and polite nation. They are anxious to learn any new project or thing they take a fancy to. They are also anxious to introduce all the European ideas into their habits and customs. Their soldiers, I am sorry to say, are not well drilled, or are not up to the mark, although they have assumed different costumes of several European nations. The Japanese seem to like the Europeans, and imitate their manners and customs. The Europeans are passionately fond of them and the country. Some of the men have distinctly told me that there is no country in the world that could equal Japan, and they would never think of returning to their homes, which they think is in no way equal to the one where they are now living. What induces them to say so is a mystery to me. As for my part, I found it very dull and quiet, although the country is very picturesque, the climate deliciously good, and people pleasant to deal with. Amongst other curious sights of Japan are their theatres and lecture rooms, where the audience has to squat on the ground, covered with common date matting. The musicians have their seats on a scaffold erected in the room, beating the drums, and playing the banjo and flute at irregular intervals.

Another curiosity is their "Jinrickshaws," a vehicle for people to move about in. In this country horses and carriages are not much known, even among the well-to-do people; jinrickshaws are much used. This vehicle resembles an ordinary Bengal buggy; the difference between them is that the former is built on a small scale and dragged by a man, instead of by a horse—a novel sight for a stranger. On enquiry as to this mode of conveyance, I was informed that horses do not live long here, the climate of this country being too cold for them; an argument which I could not believe, for horses and ponies can endure more cold and heat than any human being. These jinrickshaw men are very hard-working people. They could stand any amount of fatigue and travel in many instances as quickly and accomplish the same distance as a horse. In Yokohama and other towns, men are employed to metal and press the roads, convey huge bales on carts, instead of bullocks or horses.

As for morality, I must leave Japan out of the map altogether, for the men on this side of the world do not understand the meaning of the word "morality;" in fact, they have no such word in their dictionary. I wish the present Mikado will open his eyes and work reform among his subjects, which will be an everlasting boon, and his name shall be preserved in gold letters for future generations. I shall only say I was shocked at the dreadful way the immoralities were carried on in this country. No country is so base as Japan in this respect.

I arrived in Shanghai, and put up at the Astor House Hotel, situated near the landing-place, an American settlement.

Shanghai is situated on the river Whampoo, a tributary of the river Yangtse Kiang, and twelve miles distant from Woosung, the entrance of the Whampoo. The city is divided into four parts by river creeks, which could be crossed by bridges. The first is called the American Settlement, or commonly known as the Hankew; the English and French Settlements; and the Native Town.

The first three foreign settlements are pleasantly situated on the banks of the river; the buildings are entirely built of stone, and have a charming appearance when coming up the river. In this city all foreign powers are represented by their consuls.

The principal places I visited were the Hankew, Jessifield, Setawi, Bubbling Well, and the Race-course.

The leading banks and merchants' offices are all situated on the Yangtse Road. On the English Settlement there are about three thousand European population and twelve Parsees living at Shanghai.

As I expected, the Chinese city of Shanghai was filthy and dirty when I visited that quarter. Their joss houses (places of worship), theatres, gambling houses, and opium restaurants were all visited by me, and I was disappointed with each and all, and found them void of interest. The Chinese seem to like

European ideas well, for on entering one of their clubs, I saw that billiards, ball-alley, cards, and other games were played.

There are glass, paper, and cotton mills in Shanghai, though not in full working order; still they are trying to cultivate these industries in their country.

The foreigners have established water, gas, electric light, and other important works, and have improved the part they inhabit materially. I stayed in Shanghai for one week, and started for Hong Kong by the Messageries Maritime mail steamer, "Oxus," Captain Raphael. This line of steamers is well known for the comfortable accommodation afforded to passengers, and for the liberal table. This steamer in particular was a splendid vessel. I arrived in Hong Kong after a voyage of three days.

Victoria, the capital of Hong Kong, is built on the north-western part of the island, and follows the coast line for over three miles, and is entirely surrounded by lofty hills. The situation of the place called Praga, where the mercantile colonists have their godowns and dwelling-houses, is magnificent, and buildings are mostly built of granite. The private residences are situated on hill sides, rising, tier upon tier, to the height of several hundred feet. The appearance of these long rows of splendid buildings is strikingly effective, and gave a beautiful view while entering and leaving the harbour, which at once reminded me of the scene at Naples.

Roads leading to these fine mansions are lined with trees, and wind up the hill-side from terrace to terrace; and in some places large gardens, filled with floral wealth, is perceived, and gave a charming view. In this city the places worth visiting were the City Hall, the Clock Tower, the Government House, the Garden and Cricket Ground, the Public Gardens, the Happy Valley, the Victoria Peak, and drive from east to west points leading over the hill.

The City Hall contains a commodious and well-arranged theatre, a library, and a small museum. In the quadrangle of this hall stands a monument, richly carved, a gift of John Dent, the great merchant prince of that city.

Directly opposite the Padder Wharf stands the Clock Tower, with a fine illuminated clock.

The Government House is situated and surrounded charmingly by picturesque gardens. It is near the Public Gardens, and one hundred and fifty feet above the sea level, commanding an extensive view of the harbour and opposite coast.

The Parade and Cricket Grounds are between the City Hall and Murray Barracks, and are well kept.

Next to Government House is the Public Garden, a noteworthy object of Hong Kong, it is beautifully situated at a height of about one hundred and fifty feet above the sea, and is admirably laid out.

The Happy Valley is surrounded by hills from all sides, and is a lovely spot, full of verdure, fruits, and flowers. Here are the European and Parsee Cemeteries, all beautifully laid out; in fact, it is as good as the Public Gardens of Hong Kong. Next to the Cemetery is the Race Course, where races are annually held.

The last place I visited was the Victoria Peak, a trip I never enjoyed so immensely as this. The Peak is situated at about eighteen hundred feet high, and reached by riding in a sedan chair, carried by four coolies. A magnificent view of the harbour, the opposite mainland, the small town of Kowloon, and the surrounding islands, is to be had from this point. After staying on the Peak for an hour, and seeing the Signal Station, whence guns are fired upon the arrival of English and French mails, I returned to the town through the Reservoir and Pok Foolum (a lake). Saw some beautiful gardens belonging to Parsee and European residents.

Next day I visited the curiosity shops on the Queen's Road. In some of these the articles were displayed in fine style, and I was much struck on inspecting their embroideries on silk and satin, richly carved ivory fans, ornaments, jewel boxes, walking sticks of ebony, horn, ivory, and bamboo, gold bangles, ear-rings, scarf pins, all of delicate and intricate workmanship. Chinese work in silver is very interesting.

Many of the native shops have signs as advertisements of their wares. It is after the fashion of European retail merchants. Some of the street hawkers and other vendors of sundry articles are also sights worth seeing.

The Chinese funeral and marriage processions are frequently seen in the streets. They clothe themselves in white while in mourning, and in red for marriage festivities. The procession is formed in the same way as is done by the natives of India, with musicians, and coolies carrying a good many articles of bridal presents, walking in front of the procession.

The Chinese, as generally known, are a very hard-working and industrious race, but very dirty, and the native quarter of the town is really abominable.

Next day I visited the little town called Kowloon, on the opposite side of Hong Kong. At the extreme south of this island are handsome European residences, and a club is built, and numerous gardens are laid in this place, and the building belonging to a Parsee gentleman is charmingly situated on the sea-side. This is a favourite resort of Europeans in summer months. A steam ferry plies between Hong Kong and Kowloon.

After completing my sight-seeing in Hong Kong,

I started by the Hong Kong, Canton, and Macao Steam Navigation Company's steamer, "Powau," Captain Cary, to Canton, a distance of about ninety-four miles. These steamers are large and very comfortable. I arrived there after steaming for about nine hours.

Canton is the capital of the province of Kwantung, and the important commercial metropolis of China. The chief attractive feature of this town is a small place called Shameen, an artificial island, inhabited by Europeans. It is charmingly laid out with handsome buildings and beautiful gardens. In the interior of the city the traveller's attention is attracted to a fire temple, which contains some five hundred genii, and some other images, the Ox Flour Mills, and shops of silk ware.

I should not omit to mention that while going through the interior of the city, I was disgusted to see living rats hung up by their tails on bamboos, and other objects, such as dead cats, offered for sale; this was really a disagreeable sight.

Canton exports a large quantity of tea, silk, sugar, and a few other articles, to foreign ports. The entrance to the Canton River is very picturesque. About twelve miles distant from Canton, on the river, is a small place called Whampoo, a safe and commodious anchorage for shipping. Here we saw the Chinese forts and gunboats. I returned to Hong Kong the next day, and started next morning for

Macao, a picturesque town belonging to the Portuguese. The best portion of the town is its sea walls stretching along the Praga Grande for a mile, and a row of good substantial buildings are built on it. The interior of the town is old and shabby-looking, and void of any interest. The principal sights in Macao are the Garden and Grotto, Camoens, Military Club, Church and Hospital. When in Macao, I did not fail to visit some of the gambling houses, which are kept on a grand scale and under the direct authority of the Portuguese Government, the Government receiving a modest sum of one hundred thousand to one hundred and fifty thousand dollars annually for such permits. I returned to Hong Kong the same evening, and started the next day by the Araton Apcar Company's steamer "Japan" (Captain J. Gardiner) for Singapore.

I should not omit to mention that the beautiful harbour of Hong Kong is a safe and commodious asylum for shipping in the Eastern seas. It is surrounded by picturesque hills, and the general view while leaving and entering the harbour is magnificent, and resembles very much the bay of Naples. The view of Victoria from the harbour is charming on a dark clear night, nearly three miles of unbroken chain of gaslights stretches along the thoroughfares, and every one of the hill residences are illuminated with gas, producing a beautiful effect at night. In the harbour nearly twenty-five thousand Chinese live entirely in small boats called junks, and earn a scanty subsistence by fishing, and by carrying cargo and passengers to and from the shore. The men and women are hard-working and industrious creatures. I started for Singapore on Thursday, the 14th February, at five p.m., and passed the Green Island Lighthouse. The passage between Hong Kong and Singapore, a distance of about fourteen hundred and eighty miles, was a charming one, and accomplished in five and a half days. Captain and Mrs. Gardiner made our passage very comfortable, and I really admire their zeal and general hospitable feeling, for which they are so popular and well-known amongst the folks of Hong Kong and Calcutta.

We arrived in Singapore on the 19th February at nine p.m., and went alongside the Wharf. The island of Singapore is separated from the territory of Johore by a narrow strait about a mile in width, which occupies the southern extremity of the Malay Peninsula. The places of interest are the Raffle Square, with its adjacent quays and streets; the Raffle Library and Museum, the former of which contains about ten thousand volumes. The Botanical Garden at Tangha is a place worth visiting, where some thousands of flower plants can be seen. The garden is well kept. The Government Offices.

City Hall, and the Singapore Club are fine buildings. Malays and Khugs are the two chief inhabitants of the port, yet all other nations of the world are well represented here. Singapore is well off for docks. The Tanjoong Pagga Docks lie about a mile to the westward of the town. The climate of Singapore is warm, but the daily rainfall tempers the heat. Fruits and vegetables are obtained in abundance, and are very delicious.

I stayed in Singapore for two days, and left for Penang, arriving there after a run of thirty hours ; on the same way we passed Broom Island and the Strait Lighthouse, which is built amidst the ocean on iron frame work.

Penang, or Prince of Wales Island, is situated on the west coast of the Malay Peninsula. The chief town of Penang is George Town, but it is universally known as Penang. It is a common coaling station for the steamers and men of war. The town is built on the plains at the back of which the hills rise. The chief attraction of this district is the Waterfall, which can be reached after a splendid drive of five miles, through thickly shaded palm and beetlenut trees. While entering the harbour of Penang, I had the pleasure of witnessing many islands entirely covered with palm trees. I also here saw some fields full of beetle leaves, which the Malays and Indians eat in great quantities. We stayed in Penang two days, and left for Calcutta on the morning of the 25th February, 1884. The temperature of Penang is not the same as that of Singapore. We arrived at Calcutta on the 4th March, where I spent eight days in visiting the Exhibition and all the interesting places, and left for my Indian tour, visiting Lucknow, Cawnpore, Benares, Delhi, Lahore, Umritsar, Agra, Jeypore, Ajmere, Ahmedabad, Baroda, Surat, Bombay, and landed once more, through God's mercy, in the best of spirits and health in Kurachi, after a most interesting, delightful, and picturesque tour of twelve months Round the World.

I must add, before finishing this diary, that the courtesy, hospitality, and kindness I met throughout my travels at the hands of English, Germans, and Americans, are beyond my power to describe, and I have not sufficient words to express my deep sense of gratitude to them for making my tour so pleasant, and which ended in such great success.

THE END.

SIMMONS & BOTTEN, Printers, Shoe Lane, London.

www.ingramcontent.com/pod-product-compliance
Lightning Source LLC
Chambersburg PA
CBHW032101230426
43672CB00009B/1600